PITCHING. ISN'T. COMPLICATED.

THE SECRETS OF PRO PITCHERS AREN'T SECRETS AT ALL

BY DAN BLEWETT

PRODUCED BY LUCAS COOK

FOREWORD BY ALAN JAEGER

- Dedication -

For the first 18 years of my life, I played baseball. In the last 10 years, I've worked at it. I created this body of work but I did not do so alone. Great mentors, coaches and friends built me strong enough to endure what often felt insurmountable.

Thank you for picking me up, dusting me off, and, at times, holding my hand.

Mom, Dad, JD and Annie

Fred Cantor, Lucas Cook, Bob Gildea, Tim O'Brien, John Duffy, John Jancuska, Bob Mumma, Brooks Carey, Hal Lanier, Tim Johnson, Pete LaCock, Andy McCauley, Roye Templeton, Alan Jaeger, Nick Tumminello, Dennis and Dory Crawford, Doug Simunic, Duane Rhine, John Swanson, Steve Ekhoff, John Resta, Andrew Sacks, Scott Peddicord, Mike Laluna, Fred Dimpfel, Zach Clark, Ryan Morse, Tom Jackson, Pat Guttman, Matt Coburn, Mike Hughes, Jon Hart.

And lastly, to my family of young athletes at Warbird Training Academy: You add immeasurable purpose to my life. Thank you for trusting me.

TABLE OF CONTENTS

- Foreword -
Alan Jaeger

It is a great honor to be asked by Dan to write the foreword for his first book, Pitching Isn't Complicated. The title is apt -- Dan has taken the very broad field of "training and development" and condensed it into very clear, concise and effective principles that really get to the core of a pitchers development. What's really nice about this book is that topics go well beyond the fundamental aspects of training (mechanics, throwing programs and strength and conditioning) and delve into such intricate topics as pitch sequencing, pitch flight, holding runners on base, and how to maximize practice be it catch, flat ground or a bullpen session.

Dan is truly a passionate teacher and person who takes great interest in helping players optimize their physical and mental skills both on and off the playing field. Having played at a high level, Dan brings an incredible amount of experience as an effective coach because he's been down the path of professional baseball, and he's had to deal with the hardship of coming back from two surgeries. This experience, along with Dan's determination to find out the "why" behind pitching, arm training, strength and conditioning and mental game development has given him the ability to relate pro-level concepts to kids of all ages.

I was fortunate to meet Dan a few years ago when he flew into Los Angeles to train with us and knew right away that he was much more than just a great pitcher with a great arm -- he was extremely interested in understanding pitching and training on a much deeper level. He came with an open mind with regard to our approach, which included mental training, yoga and long toss, and not surprisingly, he took to this aspect of training with great passion, determination and interest -- and a truly open mind. I've found that the best teachers seem to be the ones with an open mind and a deep yearning to learn.

Over the past few years, Dan and I have stayed in touch and some of the constants I've noticed about him is his determination to make a difference in his students' lives by continuing to learn, and by addressing key principles that are fundamental to any athletes development. I believe this is one of the reasons why Pitching Isn't Complicated is so valuable to players, coaches and parents -- it teaches you that one of the secrets of optimizing your ability is focusing on the core principles and practicing them with high focus correctly, and, most importantly, consistently. This can significantly help leave the athlete with a clear head so he or she can train efficiently and effectively, and put time and energy into what really matters.

"The main thing is to keep the main thing, the main thing."
-Nate Trosky

Before We Get Started...
A Word on Practice Methodology

Scap-Loading? Late-Cocking? Kinetic Sequencing? Inverted W?

These are all terms that now describe or refer to pitching mechanics. As a private pitching coach, I know that they confuse both the parents and athletes.

Do I teach these principles? Some. Do I use these terms? Rarely.

I watch hundreds of thousands of throws per year, read the research and the teachings of the industry's best. What do I do next? I sift. I sift through the impractical. I sift through the ineffective. I sift through the overly complex. I sift through the old-wisdom and I sift through the fads.

On the other side of that tunnel, I've come out clean with the best drills, the simplest explanations and a clear view of how to produce not just the powerful, repeatable pitching mechanics that everyone wants, but a pitcher complete in body and mind. Good mechanics are just part of the equation. Knowing how to practice and compete are crucial but overlooked fundamentals that too often take a back seat to mechanics. We need to address the pitcher as a whole, not in parts.

In this book, I'm going to make it clear how you can perfect your pitching mechanics, allowing you to throw more strikes with more velocity. I will also discuss all of the mental aspects that are even more important than mechanics. I'll do this in simple terms that you'll understand. I don't want you to come away with a fancy new vocabulary. Rather, I want to send you on your way with a holistic knowledge of pitching, drills you can use on Monday, and lessons you will continue to use 10 years from now in your third season of pro ball. The old adage is, "if you really understand it, you should be able to explain it quickly in plain speaking." I hope to do exactly that.

This book is written for coaches, parents, instructors, and the pitchers themselves. If you're a pitcher, you need to place yourself into the role of "student." I will teach all of you how to instruct drills and mechanics, and how to perform them yourself. Every good pitcher is his own pitching coach. If you cannot teach yourself how to make changes in the middle of the game, you will never succeed. Pitchers have an instructive inner-monologue on the mound:

"Okay, you left that ball up. Break your hands a bit earlier and get on top of this next one. Let's get this hitter!"

This book will provide a comprehensive view on how to instruct yourself and others on the essential aspects of pitching.

At my facility, Warbird Training Academy, we have a clear vision based on simple, easily learned movements. The teaching philosophy and the drills that I prescribe are based on the following:

Replication of Mechanics

The aim of any mechanics drill is to ultimately instill a permanent change in ones mechanics. To do this, the drill must closely mimic the mechanical properties one wishes to have. The best drills are those that look the most like the finished product.

Mechanical Dilution & The Drill-Mound Continuum

The most important thing to keep in mind is that any mechanical change will occur over time; my term for this is mechanical dilution. Over time, high doses of the new mechanics will dilute the old mechanics, until finally new completely overtakes the old.

While perfect practice is important, at first it's only realistic at the drill level, not the throwing level. If I teach a student to make a change in the way he throws, I will first teach it without a ball, if possible. This typically results in near-100% compliance – he can do the drill perfectly. Put a ball in his hand, however, and compliance with the drill decreases; he can't do it while focusing on the drill and throwing. There is a continuum that we must consider – the drill-mound continuum.

DRILL   LIGHT CATCH   FAST CATCH   BULLPEN   MOUND

The more the student performs his drills perfectly at the low end of the continuum, the sooner and more concretely those changes will transfer to higher ends of the continuum. While a student may pick up a drill with great ease, there is almost no chance he will be able to immediately apply it at competition intensity. One needs to understand this and be patient with the learning process, understanding that it takes time, consistent drillwork and consistent, but not overbearing, coaching.

Compliance with Prescribed Drills

The term "compliance" is used to refer to two things – how well a student can physically perform a given task, and how motivated he is to continue that task as prescribed. We need drills that a student both is motivated to perform, and can perform correctly. This is what we deem 100% compliance, and it's what we need to see improvement. There are a few different reasons a student may not comply with a drill or activity I ask him to perform.

Problem: Difficulty Level

If the drill is too easy or too difficult, the student will become bored or frustrated and will give up on the drill. I thus try to make sure drills are adequately challenging to hold the attention of the student. However, as proficiency increases, all drills become relatively easy; this is the nature of drillwork. When all drills become easy, then we must employ different tactics to maintain compliance.

Solution: Explanation

The student must truly believe that a drill is essential to his career. If he believes this, the difficulty, or lack thereof, will become irrelevant. We, as coaches, want easy drills. Why? Because easy drills can be repeated thousands of times without breaking a sweat. And if we are to achieve master-status over that 10,000-hour mark, we need drills that aren't physically and mentally exhausting. Would you rather walk 10,000 miles barefoot, or in padded shoes? We want the best of both worlds – easy but effective.

But, if easy is boring, then we need to instill our reasoning for prescribing the drill so that the student is continuously motivated to remain compliant. An easy to understand, simple and relatable explanation is what is needed. This book is that explanation.

Problem: Overly Technical

Giving a student a very complex drill to perform, or multiple simple drills or pointers at the same time, will lead to lower compliance. Asking a student to perform X, Y and Z all at once leads to confusion and frustration. And, it doesn't give credit to an athletic student who very well could be proficient at all three tasks if given individually.

Especially with young pitchers, their problems are larger and require more conscious thought, thought that will negatively affect the rest of their delivery. Very advanced, elite pitchers make changes that are very subtle, often imperceptible to the untrained eye. They can make these changes in concert with others because of how small they are, and how well-trained the pitcher is. It's important to know the athlete, above all, and gauge what he can or cannot do.

Solution: Layering

The magic number of things to work on in any session is two. But, I don't necessarily ask the student to do both at the same time. Often I will layer them:

Instructor: "I want you to focus on X for the first 30 throws (the instructor monitors progress). Okay. You've done well. Now, I want you to focus on Y for the next 30 throws (the instructor monitors). Okay. That was good. Now, I want you to finish the session and make sure you're doing both X and Y, as best you can."

Problem: Space

Many students will fail to comply with their drills because they don't have a workspace in which they can be autonomous and comfortable. Compliance goes up when the student has access to a private or semi-private space where he can feel unbothered by the world, can listen to music or generally exist in his own skin.

Solution: Make Space

Set aside a space in the garage, basement, shed, or wherever that can be dedicated to the student. "Man cave" retreats are all the rage these days, and for good reason – they allow the male animal to be himself, away from the judging eye of society. If this atmosphere is fostered, the student will find himself visualizing game situations during drills, talking himself up (a technique discussed in chapter 12) and further connecting himself to his mechanics and the game. A distracting, uncomfortable environment does not provide this. The more excited a student is to be in his space, the more likely and often he will do his drills there.

Problem: Big Problems

For those with big mechanical problems, the less throwing they do while making a specific change, the better; this relates to the drill-mound continuum. Drills are less effective when they are wildly different from in-game mechanics, and as such more will be required to allow the student to shift upward the drill-mound continuum. The best solution is to ask the student not to throw at all, so he won't be negatively diluting the drill mechanics with his old, ineffective mechanics. This, however, is wildly impractical for most times of the year.

Solution: Restrictions

A high volume of drills for this population is needed, but a student will almost never shut himself down completely from throwing if he isn't already (it is recommended that two months out of the year are rest months, with no throwing whatsoever). So, we must heavily reinforce one or two changes that can be made while throwing. One tactic is forcing the student to perform drilled throws (discussed in chapter 13). I have restricted students from using anything but drilled throws for months, because I knew they would revert if I allowed them to use the windup or stretch. I do this with every student to some degree, but it's even more important for these students with major flaws.

In an ideal world, a student would perform 10,000 drills without throwing a ball; this would positively dilute his mechanics before even touching a baseball, and increase the positive change. However, since this isn't fun for the student, we have to strike a balance. What's ideal in theory is neither realistic nor practical.

Overcoaching

I don't like to overcoach, nor do my students like being overcoached. Compliance with drills will increase over time, but I feel that there is a limit to how often a student should be corrected, even if it's in his best interest.

What does overcoaching look like? It depends on the difficulty of the drill and the skill of the student. I won't provide a formula for how much coaching is too much (because I don't have one), but the idea is to point out flaws every few reps, not every single time. Additionally, the student's body language will tell you when it's time for some positive reinforcement, or simply to shut up and let him throw.

One method I have found effective is the utilization of non-verbal cues. A "cue" is a specific signal given to elicit a certain behavior. Cues are important; some work and some don't. Non-verbal cueing is less intrusive to the student, has less negative connotations and is very quick and precise; one can signal "your arm should look like this" by simply raising his or her arm in the desired manner. I will be providing the best cues for each of the drills you'll find in this book.

Lifelong vs. "Feel" Drills

The 10,000-hour idea is a very prominent one, with numerous books on the market spouting the idea that almost anyone who practices enough (10,000 hours or so) will achieve expert-level skill at that activity. I agree – repetition is the single most important factor in getting really good at something.

Some drills are intended for continued use throughout ones career to maintain compact, repeatable mechanics. Others are meant to teach how a new change feels, and once that feel is achieved, the drill is shelved. It's important to know the difference, because we want to maximize practice time, and thus carryover of drills to on-field performance. Feel drills ideally improve the quality of repetitions performed in a lifelong drill.

You should put a handful of lifelong drills in your back pocket and use them throughout your career. These drills should help reset and get you back on track when you feel out of sync or uncomfortable on the mound. They should also strongly resemble what you deem are "perfect" pitching mechanics. If you practice mechanics that are perfect, every repetition will get you closer to perfection.

The Starting Point

My method is not bottom-up. I start my students somewhere in the middle, at a drill that I feel most good athletes should be able to perform. This way, they feel challenged right off the bat. If they fail to succeed with the drill, then I make it simpler and easier, and then reintroduce as proficiency increases. I've found it best not to start at the very simplest drill, but to start in the middle, assess, and then move forward or backward as is appropriate.

I don't want anyone to blindly follow. I want readers to follow because the value in my teachings is obvious and actionable. The way to get others to believe is to explain– fully, clearly, and repeatedly. When those I train bring conflicting advice, I don't dismiss it. If I disagree, I will give reasons why. I know that everything I teach, everything that is in this book, holds up to scrutiny. This is only because I have tried so much myself and weighed the pros and cons of other methods. Everything in this book will provide the maximum effect with the minimum dose.

There are many different ways to pitch, as seen in the Major Leagues – no two pitchers have exactly the same mechanics or pitch the same way. But, as I will outline for you, there are maxims, archetypes that every good pitcher tends to follow. These are the ones to which you should pay most attention. "Works for you" is fine until it no longer gets you where you want to go. If you're not going where you want to go, or are not as good as you want to be, then this book is for you.

CHAPTER 1

THE WIND UP

The wind up should be used by all starting pitchers. A simple, efficient wind up utilizing as few steps as possible will produce consistency in the pitching delivery and produce maximum velocity. Keeping the head stable and body balanced are the most important aspects of a good wind up.

Pre-Pitch Set-Up

Important Terminology – Armside & Gloveside:
To eliminate lefty/righty confusion, I will speak of the rubber, the plate, and other matters in this book as armside or gloveside. On one side of the body resides the pitcher's throwing arm (armside), and one side resides his glove arm (gloveside). Using this terminology makes things much simpler.

Where to Set Up on the Rubber

Finding the ideal pre-pitch stance depends on a few factors. Most important is the shape of ones breaking ball, which is determined by the type of pitch, arm slot and hand action. Other factors include the rest of the pitcher's arsenal and his specific strengths and weaknesses.

When you settle on the perfect spot for you, pay attention to your drive foot – it's the target for the recommendations below. So, if you choose to use the gloveside third of the rubber, your drive foot (the one that pivots in contact with the rubber) should be the foot that's in your newly chosen spot (more on this below).

Set up in the center third of the rubber if:
- You throw a 12-6 curveball
- You throw your fastball to each side of the plate with equal success/difficulty
- Your armslot is ¾, high-¾ or over the top.

Set up on the gloveside third of the rubber if:
- You throw a sinker as your primary fastball
- Your arsenal is primarily fastball/changeup
- You struggle to make pitches on the gloveside of edge of the plate

Set up on the armside third of the rubber if:
- You throw a slider, 1-7 curveball or slurve
- You have a low-¾, sidearm or submarine arm slot
- You struggle to make pitches on the armside of edge of the plate

<u>Why This Recommendation is Ideal</u>

Breaking Ball Shape

The shape of ones breaking ball and his ability to throw it for a called strike is very important. A sharp breaking ball is produced by releasing the pitch directly out in front of the body with great extension and second knuckle forward of the ball.

Breaking pitch with second knuckle on top
and in front of the ball.

Consider a hypothetical pitcher who throws a slider that breaks seven inches laterally. He sets up on the gloveside of the rubber. If he releases the pitch out in front, where will it end up after breaking seven inches? The answer is between five and seven inches off the plate (for a ball – see number 1 in the accompanying illustration). Thus, this pitcher, to throw his slider for a strike, would have to release the pitch slightly behind his body, which would result in reduced spin, causing a softer-breaking, "hanging" slider.

We want the set point for breaking balls to be down the middle for a strike so that the called-strike breaking ball is a sharp one. Then, when it's time to bury one down and off the plate, the pitcher only has to pull harder down on the pitch at release. This setup on the rubber gives the pitcher an advantage – it will be easier to throw consistently sharper breaking balls.

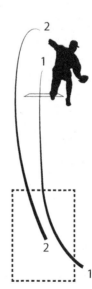

Pitch "1," thrown out in front with sharp, late break, will result in a ball.

Pitch "2," in order to be thrown for a strike, must be released behind the pitcher's head, which results in softer, less effective break.

Commanding Both Sides of the Plate

Rubber placement can also greatly affect a pitcher's command. If a pitcher struggles to locate fastballs gloveside, for instance, it may be beneficial to set up more on the gloveside third of the rubber. The converse can be true – if a pitcher struggles to throw strikes on the armside of the plate, he may benefit from setting up more on the armside of the rubber. This can allow him to more effectively move the ball to both sides of the plate, rather than being skilled at only one side.

Lateral and Sinking Movement

Those who throw sinkers and/or rely on their changeup as an out-pitch are better off using the gloveside third of the rubber. While we want breaking balls to be released out in front, pitchers get more later movement and sink on changeups and two-seam fastballs when their hand and arm lag slightly behind. By lag, I mean that the hand isn't quite at the top of the arm swing with the forearm vertical, ready to accelerate forward. This slight lag results in the hand turning over late, produce more rollover of the hand and arm, which curtails backspin and produces more overspin and sidespin.

For the above reason, changeups and fastballs thrown on the armside of the plate will have more lateral and sinking movement. Thus, when pitchers move to the gloveside of the rubber, balls thrown to the middle of the plate will act like those thrown on the armside half, and those thrown on the armside half will have even more drastic movement. This adjustment on the rubber simply lets the sinker/changeup pitcher use more of the plate with high effect.

Arm Slot

The lower the arm slot, the more lateral break we will see on a slider or curveball. This is a major factor as addressed above. Additionally, with low-3/4, side-arm and submarine arm slots, the pitcher wants to take advantage of the behind the hitter effect. With a low arm slot, every pitch, fastball included, has the appearance of starting behind hitters of the same handedness (the main reason lefty-lefty and right-righty matchups are manipulated by managers). It's very difficult for a hitter to track a pitch that ap-

pears to start behind him. Thus, for lower arm slot pitchers, it is advantageous to set up on the armside third of the rubber, to increase the natural sweep of their pitches across the plate.

Conflicting Pitch Shapes

Although the recommendations for proper placement on the rubber apply to most pitchers, they may not work for everyone. Often, we need give and take when a pitcher throws pitches that conflict with one another, such as the sinker and slider. Because a majority of sinker pitchers also throw a slider (the typically lower arm slot is conducive to both pitches) it may be wise to experiment with different rubber locations. I feel that the slider is best thrown from the armside third of the rubber, but the sinker is best thrown from the gloveside third. So, pitchers with both offerings may need to strike a balance, because pitchers need to throw from the same spot every time, regardless of the pitch. Moving on the rubber on a pitch by pitch basis is not advised.

The Steps of The Wind Up

Wind Up Terminology:

Lead Foot: The foot that will descend down the mound toward the hitter.
Lead Leg: The leg that will lift into the leg kick and descend down the mound
Drive Foot: The foot that will contact the rubber and provide a base for the leg kick
Drive Leg: The leg that will support the body and remain in contact with the rubber
Leg Kick: The act of lifting the lead leg up into the air to gather and release energy
Hand Break: When the hand holding the ball separates from and leaves the glove
Landing Position or Foot Strike: When the pitcher has reached full stride and reconnects with the mound

Step 1: Stance

Stand on the rubber with your feet at shoulder-width, half on the rubber and half in front. I suggest that the hands are held slightly out in front of the chest.

Why this is the ideal method:
I like the hands in front of the chest because it's the most neutral position as the hands break. The

23

throwing hand will move down after breaking from the glove, and finally up into the high cocked position before traveling forward. A happy middle ground between these two points is the chest – if you were to bisect the arc of the arm swing, the chest would be very near the middle. Additionally, having the hands near the chest allows clearance from a high leg kick; those who carry their hands low often have to move them up, anyway, as the leg kick rises. A shoulder-width stance provides extra balance and gives ample foot clearance for the subsequent steps in the sequence.

Starting wider also simplifies an extra step – the sideways or backward step that most pitchers use to begin their motion is typically much larger than Step 2 of our wind up, which causes both an off-center weight shift and movement of the head – both major pitfalls that we wish to avoid.

Keeping the center of mass stable provides the pitcher with greater balance, which in turn leads to less variability in the leg lift and stride, thereby producing a more consistent release point.

Keeping the head stable allows the eyes to stay locked on their target, and we need the eyes locked on the target so that the body will follow. Less head movement means a more stable center of mass and more consistent movement of the chest and arm toward the target.

Step 2: Lead foot steps forward to land at 45°

Why this is the ideal method:

Stepping forward at 45° makes sense for the following reasons:

1. *Foot Plant Consistency*. The mound is almost always the flattest and best kept in the area a few inches forward of the rubber. Stepping backward or sideways leads one closer to the slope of the mound, which is more often poorly groomed. Stepping down the slope, into holes and on rocks will cause a major weight-shift, making the pitcher's windup unpredictable. Cleats can easily get snagged while stepping over the rubber and in and out of these poorly groomed areas. Professional mounds are very consistent, but amateur mounds are often poorly constructed and groomed, and thus it can be disastrous should one step too far away from the rubber.

2. ***Center of Mass stays stable.*** Stepping backward or to the side will cause the weight to shift and the head to move. Both of these are flaws that will create poor tracking of the eyes and body toward the target.

3. ***Partial Hip Turn.*** The hips need to turn 90° from starting position, and stepping forward at 45° makes it significantly easier to then complete this rotation as the drive foot pivots to the rubber in Step 3.

Step 3: Drive foot pivots against the rubber

This step needs little explanation. One note, however – the pitcher needs to pick the foot up, not just pivot. Pivoting with cleats makes for a clunky movement; cleats often snag in holes, on rocks and in the dirt in general. This seems obvious but many amateur pitchers will practice this incorrectly indoors by pivoting their foot without lifting it.

Step 4: Leg lifts to 90° or higher torso angle

I have found that when pitchers want to throw harder, they lift their leg both higher and faster. This is consistent across my very large sample of pitchers who throw at maximal effort for 8-12 weeks in my winter program.

I thus recommend that a pitcher allow his leg to kick as high as is comfortable. Too high will result in poor balance and consistency, but 90° relative to the torso, or higher, is my recommendation.

As the leg lifts, the body will tend to coil backward, showing the butt and back slightly to the plate. A small degree of this coiling (also known as wrapping or spinning) is normal and acceptable, but higher degrees make it difficult to land straight toward the target, which makes pitching down and to the gloveside of the strike zone difficult. I suggest that the body stays as square to the plate as possible, with the chest and torso perpendicular to the plate.

FAQ – *I've been taught to point my toe down during my leg kick so that I can more reliably land on my forefoot as I stride. Is this correct?*

Pointing the toe down is irrelevant because almost no one actually lands on his toe. Upon observing the landing position of almost any MLB pitcher, one will see the heel initiating contact with the ground. While this fix would make sense, it's simply not going to happen – you will land on your heel regardless of the effort to point the toe down.

Reciprocal inhibition says that when a muscle fires, any muscles that oppose it must relax. It is my theory that the slope of the mound, coupled with the pattern of muscle activation responsible for extending the lead leg down the mound, is what prevents a pitcher from landing on his forefoot.

Additionally, let's not overthink every single detail. Unless there's a problem, be athletic and let your body do what it naturally wants to do. Often times what we naturally do, we do because it's efficient. This is obviously not the case in all situations, but again – be an athlete first.

Step 5: Hands break immediately as leg descends

Ideal hand break can start slightly before the leg descends, but most often the hands will break and swing upward at the same pace that the leg lift descends down and forward.

A common flaw that causes the arm to drag, and, subsequently, pitches up in the zone, is a late hand break. The hands, if broken too late, will not have adequate time to ascend to the proper height to apply maximal force and create ideal hand position. This is addressed in detail in chapter five.

One way of conceptualizing this is by analogy. Imagine the baseball is an egg – as the leg lifts, crack the egg on your knee, then go on and finish the rest of the delivery. Tim O'Brien, one of my mentors in college, taught this analogy.

The Trouble with Other Methods

Hands Above the Head

My answer for why I don't go a la Greg Maddux is simple: simplicity. With the arms overhead, timing is essential and one must be very precise to be consistent. Additionally, speaking on anomalies in the mound, one is more likely to lose balance with a small misstep with the hands overhead than held in position around the chest. Less moving parts will yield more consistency in more pitchers, though it is certainly possible to be successful working overhead.

Feet Close Together

When an athlete in any sport wants to improve his balance and stability, the first move is to widen the stance – ask any NFL lineman. Pitching is the same way, and starting in a narrow footing adds complexity to the delivery – the feet are forced to move wider to create a more stable base. Eliminate this step by starting shoulder width or so (too wide has a similarly negative effect).

Hands Held Very High or Low

Some pitchers like to hide their face behind their mitt, and others like to hold their hands very low. Both add unnecessary movement to the delivery because the hands will want to break in a position more central to the arm swing. Some movement is necessary for timing, but again – fewer movements gives less time for things to go awry.

Spinning/Coiling/Wrapping

Wrapping the body around the back leg, also referred to as spinning or coiling, adds another dimension to the delivery that must be undone. For every degree that one coils backward (revealing the butt and back to the hitter), one must uncoil the same amount to eventually land in a straight line to the plate. Many pitchers do this – it's very common – but it can become very difficult to land straight to the plate and pitch effectively to the gloveside edge of the plate.

CHAPTER 2

THE STRETCH

The stretch is broken into two separate deliveries – the leg kick and the hybrid slide step. The hybrid slide step allows a pitcher to be very fast to the plate without loss of velocity or consistency. A leg kick is more appropriate when there are runners on second or third base with little threat of stealing. Knowing the game situation and speed of the runners will guide the pitcher in choosing the appropriate delivery from the stretch.

In the stretch position, we need two separate deliveries, one using the normal, high leg kick and one using a modified slide step. I will first address the set up common to both before explaining the difference between the two.

Pre-Pitch Set-Up

Pre-Sign

Before setting the drive foot in contact with the rubber, the pitcher must step onto the forward surface of the mound. One can do this by straddling the rubber with a very wide stance (drive foot behind the rubber) or by walking onto the forward surface and simply placing the drive foot in contact with the rubber.

Sign Set

The sign set is my term for the position one will take while receiving signs from the catcher. The sign set is simply a widened stance, with drive foot in contact with the rubber, which allows the pitcher to shorten up into the proper stance to come fully set before delivering a pitch.

Set Position

After the sign is confirmed, the pitcher will shorten up his stance into the set position. I advocate for a set position with feet spread 12"-18" apart. I feel this is ideal for the following reasons:

1. Weight can be distributed properly – about 70/30 on the drive foot
2. Feet are far enough apart to prevent them from tangling during pick off moves
3. The leg lift will be less inclined to cross over the rubber, allowing lefties to pick off to 1st base, and both righties and lefties to perform the inside move to 2nd base, without fear of balking. Balking is discussed at length in the beginning of chapter three.
4. Weight can be shifted back before going forward when the pitch is delivered. This is crucial for properly executing the slide step.

The Leg Lift

There is no distinction between the leg lift used in the wind up and the leg lift used in the stretch. We still desire at least a 90° angle relative to the torso, and the cadence of the leg lift should not change.

The Slide Step

The term "slide step" often refers to a pitcher simply picking up his front foot and driving toward the plate; I do not teach this brand of slide step because I feel it negatively affects a pitchers timing, weight shift and velocity. Although it can certainly work for some, I don't feel it is the most effective method for the majority.

My slide step is a hybrid version of normal leg kick height and slide step height, designed to provide a proper back leg load and weight shift. This version which will allow the pitcher to keep his normal rhythm and velocity while being faster to the plate. For the rest of this manual, when I refer to the slide step, I am referring to my version, the "hybrid slide step."

Performing the Hybrid Slide Step

Step 1: Assume set position as outlined above. Feet must be 12"-18" inches apart.

Step 2: Lead foot moves backward toward the rubber
• Lead foot lifts just high enough off the ground to move without catching the ground.

Step 3: Knock knees
• The knee of the lead leg should travel toward the back of the mound until it meets or surpasses the knee of the drive leg.
• Even though the foot barely leaves the ground, the lead leg will give the appearance of a half leg lift with approximately 45° angle relative to the torso.

Step 4: Go forward
• As soon as the knees knock, weight has shifted adequately and the pitcher can travel forward to the plate as fast as he feels comfortable.
• The faster the lead leg moves backward, the faster it can then come forward toward the plate. Typically, speed backward equals speed forward.

Choosing the Wind Up vs. Leg Lift vs. the Slide Step

This is not set in stone and is largely up to the pitcher. The following table contains generalizations that will apply for most pitchers most of the time.

However, the golden rule is, "Make sure a pitcher is optimally comfortable to throw the best pitch possible." If a pitcher would rather pitch from the slide step exclusively because he feels more confident and in control that way, then he has a strong case to do so.

Pitchers are typically most comfortable, in descending order:
1. Wind up (most comfortable)
2. Leg lift
3. Slide step (least comfortable)

	WIND UP	STRETCH (Leg Lift)	STRETCH (Slide Step)
BASES EMPTY	1st Choice	No	No
BASES LOADED (2 Outs)	1st Choice	2nd Choice	No
BASES LOADED (0 or 1 Out)	No	1st Choice	2nd Choice
RUNNER ON 1ST *(Fast lead runner)*	Never	No	1st Choice
RUNNER ON 1ST *(Slow lead runner)*	Never	2nd Choice	1st Choice
RUNNERS ON 1ST & 2ND *(Fast lead runner)*	Never	No	1st Choice
RUNNERS ON 1ST & 2ND *(Slow lead runner)*	Never	1st Choice	2nd Choice
RUNNERS ON 1ST & 3RD *(Fast runner on 1st)*	Never	2nd Choice	1st Choice
RUNNERS ON 1ST & 3RD *(Slow runner on 1st)*	Never	2nd Choice	1st Choice
RUNNERS ON 2ND & 3RD	2nd Choice	1st Choice	No
RUNNER ON 2ND	Never	1st Choice	2nd Choice
RUNNER ON 3RD	1st Choice	2nd Choice	No

Interpreting the Table:
1. Never – There's never a good reason to use these mechanics in this situation
2. No – It's a poor choice, given one or two better options.
3. 1st Choice – Exactly what it means
4. 2nd Choice – Exactly what it means

Reasoning Behind These Recommendations

I are considering comfort level in some of my suggestions on situational use of the three different sets of mechanics. Being comfortable is an important contributor toward being effective. Pitchers uncomfortable in their mechanics pitch with less confidence and consistency.

Bases empty: Most pitchers throw 1 or 2 mph harder from the windup. I suggest you capitalize on this.

Bases loaded, two outs: Runners are moving on the batted ball anyway, so using the slide step won't lessen the chance of a runner scoring from second on a single, and a double will clear the bases almost all the time anyway. Choose the more comfortable option.

Bases loaded, zero or one out: I suggest using the stretch to prevent runners from getting a huge jump that allows them to take an extra base on a single or double, to break up a double play, or to score from third on a ball hit to the corner infielders. Pitching from the stretch also increases the likelihood the runner on second may be cut down at the plate on a hard-hit single.

1st only with fast runner: This situation is obvious – prevent a steal of second base by using the fastest delivery to the plate. Keeping the runner on first keeps the double play in order. The slide step also makes it more difficult for the runner to go from first to third on a single to the right side.

1st only with slow runner: Holding the runner close to maintain the double play and keep him from taking third on a ball hit to the right side is a priority, even if the runner is slow.

1st & 2nd with fast lead runner: In this situation, a stolen base will hurt a lot, as both runners will move up. A double steal will happen only if the lead runner can get a great jump, so using the slide step is imperative.

1st & 2nd with slow lead runner: Even with a slow lead runner, a double steal can occur if the pitcher forgets about checking the runner on second. Going from the slide step will deter a slow runner from attempting to steal third, even if the pitcher pays inadequate attention to him.

1st & 3rd with fast or slow runner: Especially in amateur ball, teams like to try stealing second base in this situation and/or try stealing home once the throw goes through. Using the slide step will give a better opportunity to catch at least one runner.

2nd & 3rd: These runners aren't going anywhere and the double play is not in order, so there is little reason to hold these runners. The only goal is to keep the runner on second from getting a ridiculous lead. But the reality is that both runners will score on a hit and will advance with a good sacrifice fly or ball hit to the right side of the infield (if less than two out).

2nd only: This runner should be watched but is not a major threat – third base is much less likely to be stolen. If the runner is exceptionally fast and the situation is such that a steal of third is very advantageous, the slide step should be used.

3rd only: With a runner on third, the run will either be conceded on a ground ball to the middle infield or deep fly ball; the runner will hold on a ball to the pitcher, first or third, and will score on any hit. There is little reason to worry about him, and it's senseless to use the threat of stealing home as an excuse to use a less comfortable set of mechanics. Yet, using the stretch will keep the runner a few feet closer to the base, which may help cut him down on a play at the plate. But, if the stretch is much less comfortable, this benefit may not be worth it.

CHAPTER 3

PICK OFF MOVES

Pick off moves are often misunderstood – they are most often used to disrupt the timing of runners and rarely result in outs. Knowing the proper pick off moves not only gives the pitcher the best chance at picking off a lazy runner, but also controlling the running game in general. Any time a pitcher throws to a base, he should do so with the intent to get an out.

In this chapter I will address the different moves that each pitcher must have in his arsenal. The theory behind holding runners and when to use them will be discussed in Chapter Four.

If one sticks to the footwork outlined below, he will not be in violation of any balk rules. A balk is vaguely defined as an "attempt to deceive the runner." The most relevant rules regarding the balk are as follows:

1. For a righthander, once in contact with the rubber, if the lead foot moves first, he must throw to the plate. The drive foot must disconnect first from the rubber to throw to first base.
2. For a lefthander, his lead leg may lift and he may still throw to the first base so long as his foot does not cross the rubber and his weight does not shift toward the plate. Once the leg reaches its highest point, weight must go either toward the plate or to the base to pick off. An imaginary 45° line typically defines whether the step to first is legal.
3. Once set, a pitcher may only move his head; any other movement is illegal.
4. Once in motion toward the plate, the pitcher must deliver the pitch and may not stop.
5. When performing the inside move to second base, the runner must step completely over the rubber and toward second base.
6. The pitcher may not fake a throw to first base, unless he steps back off the rubber first.
7. The pitcher may fake a throw toward second or third base.
8. The pitcher may not attempt a pick off to an unoccupied base.
9. A pitcher must come to a complete stop when coming to the set position. This is usually defined as a one-second pause.

The following are the most common reasons a pitcher will balk; most result from indecision and confusion.

- **Spastic movement**. Once set, only the head can move. Sometimes the body will twitch for no real reason, resulting in a balk. Often a cleat getting snagged can lead to this.
- **Didn't stop**. Rules state that a pitcher must come to a complete stop when coming set. Many pitchers get in a rhythm and forget to come to a discernable stop.
- **Runners or fielders do something unexpected**. When pitchers are unprepared for a runner leaving early, a bunt, etc., they will often panic and twitch or stop their delivery after moving toward the plate.
- **Personal indecision**. Sometimes a pitcher considers picking off, going to the plate or changing his pitch all at once. He gets flustered and accidently twitches or stops his delivery.
- **Coaches yelling instructions**. When a pitcher is set on a single task, and the coach or catcher suddenly yells for him to do something different (often: "Step off!"), the pitcher will get confused and twitch or stop his delivery.

The Essential Moves for Righthanders

Moves Designed to Pick Off and Chase Back

Two moves are performed with the goal of, at worst, chasing the runner back, and at best, picking him off. These are the pivot move to first base and the spin move to second base. In both of these moves the pitcher should use them only with the full intent of making a hard throw to the base to catch the runner. Included in each illustration is whether or not it is legal to fake a throw to this base (performing the pivot move without throwing to first will result in a balk).

To 1st Base – The Pivot Move

(NOTE: This move <u>cannot</u> be faked.)

About this move:

It's shocking how many high school players do not know how to perform this move – they will instead step back off the rubber and then pivot to throw. There is no reason for such a slow, clunky move – it is legal for the drive foot to disconnect forward from the rubber as long as it is the first foot to move. Always make a hard throw to first, with aim set low and at the lead corner of the base.

To 2nd Base – The Spin Move

(NOTE: This move <u>can</u> be faked.)

About this move:

The spin move uses the same foot technique as the pivot move; the only difference is a much larger arc-turn to second base. It is imperative that the player stays in control – the hips need to fully clear to second base or else the throw will be far off target into the outfield gap. This move needs to be executed rapidly, but in control – consistent practice is needed to get the footwork down. This move is effective with a hard throw to the lead corner of the base or a convincing fake throw.

Moves That are Info-Gathering – NOT True Pick-Offs

The concept of "lengthening the baseline" is a good one. While true pickoff moves do the best job of keeping runners close to the base (thus increasing the distance to the next base), info-gathering moves can do the same thing. The more aware the runner is that the pitcher is thinking about him, the closer to the base he will stay.

To 2nd Base – The Inside Move

(NOTE: This move <u>can</u> be faked.)

About this move:
The inside move is too often performed lackadaisically and as such has little effect. If done well, it is very deceptive and can prove a valuable tool to catch lazy runners and gather bunt information. The pitcher must lift his leg with the same cadence and height as his normal leg lift; at the last moment he will turn toward second base instead of pitching. It is easy to master this move; most pitchers have ineffective inside moves simply because they lack the dedication to practice.

The inside move works well to exploit lazy runners – it can catch a runner running on the pitch, such as on a 3-2 count with two outs. It can also catch a runner who likes to steal on the pitcher's first movement toward the plate. But, it's not a true pick-off move in the sense that if the runner is caught by it, the pitcher is unlikely to make a throw to 2nd base – the runner will usually be well on his way to 3rd. As such, the pitcher should always be prepared to run at the base runner should he catch him in the middle of the base path. The throw should go to third base to tag the runner or capture him in a rundown. Too many pitchers perform the move well, only to be startled when the runner continues on toward third. This often results in an overthrow or the runner getting safely to third base.

The inside move is also used to determine if a hitter will be bunting. When the sacrifice bunt sign is given, the hitter will usually wait to show bunt until the pitcher lifts his leg. The inside move will reveal the hitter's intent to bunt, after which the manager will decide how to defend it. Smart pitchers use the inside move in close games with a runner on 2nd base and nobody or one out to sniff out a bunt or steal attempt.

To 3rd Base – The Third to First (*now illegal*)

About this move:
Prior to 2013, there was only one reason to pick off to third base – to pull the old third to first move to catch a runner sleeping or reveal a bunt. However, as of 2013, the third to first pickoff move for righthanders is illegal. So, in case any of you old-school coaches or ex-players didn't get the memo, don't teach this to your young players!

The Essential Moves for Lefthanders

Lefthanders should always be good at holding runners due to their natural advantage of facing the runner at first base. Any lefty who does not hold runners well is probably lazy and lacks dedication to learn the proper moves. Lefties have two moves to first base; righthanders have just one. The lefties'spin move and inside move are the same as covered for righties; however, I am providing a graphic for each move featuring lefty-specific footwork.

Moves Designed to Pick Off and Chase Back

To 1st Base - The Hang Move

About this move:
The hang move to first is the reason lefthanded pitchers can easily stifle the running game. Pitchers with effective hang moves will execute a leg lift with exactly the same height and cadence, regardless of whether they go to the plate or plan to pick-off to first. Pitchers who can keep their eyes and shoulders pointing toward the plate have the most convincing moves toward first base. When finally making their move toward first, lefties must make sure their weight does not go forward, toward the plate, and that their step is at a 45° angle or less in reference to the imaginary line drawn from the rubber to home plate.

To 1st Base - The Snap Throw

(NOTE: This move can be faked.)

About this move:

The snap throw is the only move that requires the pitcher to step back off the rubber before throwing. Because lefthanders face the runner at first base, they can observe movement and use the snap throw to make a sudden pick off to the base. The pitcher simply steps off and throws to first base as fast as he can. This throw is not typically very strong because of poor body positioning, so pitchers may struggle to make crisp throws using this move unless they have a very powerful arm.

To 2nd Base - The Spin Move

(NOTE: This move can be faked.)

Moves That are Info-Gathering – NOT True Pick-Offs

To 2nd Base - The Inside Move

(NOTE: This move can be faked.)

Moves That are Useless or Irrelevant

Righties & Lefties: The Soft-Toss Pick-Off Move

You've seen it – the pitcher makes a pick-off move to a base only to make a 30-mph rainbow throw. This does absolutely nothing to put the fear of being picked off into the runner, nor does it disrupt a runner's timing. All this move does is waste time and slow the pace of the game, which will bore the fielders, fans and hitters, and negatively affect the pitcher's rhythm. This move is completely useless and should never be implemented.

Righties & Lefties: The Step-Off and Look

Because no throw is made, this move does not put fear of being picked off into a runner, and thus will not hold him close to the base. The typical rationale for its use is, "It reminds the runner that you know he is there." Of course, the pitcher knows the runner is there – if he didn't he'd be pitching from the windup! Pick-offs should only be made with purposeful throws – stepping off should only be used as a reset if the pitcher is uncomfortable or if the fielders are out of position.

Righties Only: Picking Off to 3rd Base

An overthrow to third base results in the runner scoring – the runner has nowhere else to go, so his lead is largely irrelevant. Also, a pitcher cannot pick off to third from the wind up, which is the only time steals of home occur. So, if a pitcher is in the stretch with a runner on third, the runner isn't going to steal home, which makes it irrelevant to hold him close to third. Additionally, the third baseman will be playing away from the bag and not holding the runner, making an overthrow to very probable because the third baseman would have to catch the ball on the run. There is absolutely no sensible reason to pick off to third base.

CHAPTER 4

HOLDING RUNNERS

The running game is all about holding the ball. Hold the ball for varying lengths of time before pitching or picking off. This will make your movements difficult to predict, which will make it difficult for runners to get good jumps. Lastly, pick off with the intent to get an out.

"If a runner wants to go, he'll go. All you can do is discourage him and disrupt his timing."
                                                                                    –Hal Lanier

Holding Runners is a Fourfold Process:

1. Develop a quick delivery to the plate
2. Understand stealing situations and counts
3. Pick off at optimal moments to "protect" pitches
4. Disrupt the runner's timing

Important Youth Baseball Considerations

Before I delve into some of the more complicated situations in which a smart pitcher can help control the running game, it's important to address the fact that most youth and amateur players and coaches simply do not have a good understanding of baseball situations. When facing ignorant opponents, situational knowledge will often become irrelevant, as it must be possessed by both sides. Many runners have no clue of when a "good" time is to run – they just run with no regard to the situation. In these cases, higher learning doesn't help the pitcher because the runner doesn't play by the same rules.

So, it is important to recognize that in amateur baseball, where situational knowledge is lacking by both the offense and defense, many of the situations discussed below are only helpful preparing for elite levels of baseball. Again, if the runner doesn't know how to judge the quality of a running situation, then the pitcher has no way of playing the percentages in regards to the runners' likelihood to steal. Fortunately, the basics are effective regardless of situational knowledge: hold the ball; vary delivery times to the plate; be fast with the slide step; pick off with the intent to get an out. These maxims are effective at all levels of baseball, even when situational knowledge is lacking.

Developing a Quick Delivery to the Plate

The first step toward being quick to the plate is using proper stretch mechanics. Consult the chart in chapter two for when to use the windup, leg lift or slide step to defeat base runners. Understand that it's next to impossible to use a regular leg lift and deliver a pitch in less than 1.5 seconds, which is a slow delivery to the plate. To effectively hold runners, a pitcher must learn the hybrid slide step, which is the most comfortable way to move quickly to the plate without sacrificing velocity.

1.30 or Less is the Goal

To time the speed of a pitcher's delivery to the plate, the stopwatch starts upon his first move to the plate; we stop when his pitch hits the catchers mitt. A good catcher "pop time" at the collegiate level is 2.0 or less, which, when coupled with a pitcher delivering in 1.3 or less, gives a base runner only 3.3 seconds to travel approximately 80 feet (factoring in average lead of 10 feet). This requires a very fast runner getting a very good jump.

Coaches time opposing pitchers to determine their speed to the plate then make adjustments to their running plan accordingly. When a coach sees a pitcher use a full leg lift, or generally posts a 1.6 or higher, he will give all but his slowest runners the "green light," meaning steal at will.

Getting to the 1.3 mark will vary slightly according to age, as the flight duration of the pitch will account for about 1/3 of the pitcher's speed to the plate. A 90-mph pitcher's fastball will take approximately 0.4 seconds to travel from his hand to the plate, meaning that 0.9 seconds is the time allotted for him to release the pitch to achieve a 1.3. It becomes apparent, when factoring in pitch speed as a contributor to delivery speed, that runners will try to steal on offspeed pitches when possible, which take longer to reach the plate.

Seconds to the Plate
1.1 – Extremely fast
1.2 – Very fast
1.3 – Fast
1.4 – Average
1.5 – Below average
1.6 – Very slow
1.7+ - Extremely slow

Many pitchers seemingly ignore their speed to the plate due to ignorance or a refusal to deviate from comfortable leg lift mechanics. The fact is: Pitchers who give up stolen bases routinely give up more runs – any stolen base results in a runner in scoring position. Any pitcher would be unhappy giving up a double. Yet, these same pitchers who try hard to avoid extra-base hits regularly ignore runners and allow them to steal second or third, thereby turning walks, singles or hit-by-pitches into doubles and triples.

A single followed by a stolen base and another single will score a run; two consecutive singles does not. Being quick to the plate saves runs and forces the opposing team to work harder to earn them.

A pitcher should remind himself repeatedly: a walk and a stolen base is essentially a double. A blooper scores that double, resulting in a very cheap run. *Good pitchers don't allow cheap runs.*

Understanding Stealing Situations and Counts

If a pitcher understands situations in which runners are more likely to run, he can save his pick off attempts for moments that will have a greater effect. Most young amateur base runners haven't a clue about when to steal, and because catchers are mostly unable to catch runners, they simply run amuck. Yet, good coaches, who put the steal signs into effect, do understand situations – they will ensure that their base runners make more sensible decisions on the base paths, regardless of whether or not they understand them.

Running Situations – When They're More Likely To Steal

Fast Runners

Fast runners are often given the "green light," meaning that they can choose to steal anytime they feel capable. These runners will often steal in less-than-ideal situations, simply because they can. It is important to keep these runners close at all times, regardless of the situation.

Two Outs, Runner on First

This is a great situation for a runner to steal because, if successful, he places himself in scoring position in an otherwise dead inning. On first base, it would take two hits to score him in most cases, but a stolen base and a single will produce a quick run. While this is true with any number of outs, an attempt with less than two outs could quickly stop a potential big inning if the runner is caught. But with two outs, it's unlikely that a team will get multiple hits to score multiple runs, so the risk/reward of a steal attempt is much more favorable.

One Out, Runner on Second

Manufacturing a run refers to systematically moving a runner from base to base and/or scoring a runner without getting a base hit. With a runner on second and one out, the hitting team cannot manufacture a run. However, if the runner advances to third with one out, a sacrifice fly or ground ball to the middle infield will score the runner. Thus it's a great time to steal third if the runner can get a good jump.

It should be noted that runners are even more likely to steal third with a righthanded batter at the plate – the batter blocks the catcher's view of third base and makes an accurate throw much less likely. With a lefty at the plate, the catcher has an open lane to throw to third. It's a short throw, so without the obstruction of a righthanded hitter, it's easier to catch a runner stealing third.

Runners on First and Third

Pitchers typically pay less attention to runners on first when there's also a runner on third base. Runners get a much larger lead in this situation and as such are tempted to steal, knowing that a throw may not even go through to second base.

Weak Hitter on Deck

Base runners are less likely to steal when the team's best hitters, 2-3-4-5, are due at the plate. This is because these hitters are more likely to bat the runner in without the aid of a steal. It's a sin to get caught stealing just to have the hitter follow with a double or homerun. When less powerful hitters follow who are more likely to hit singles than extra-base hits, a stolen base attempt makes more sense – a mere single will score the run.

Understanding Pick-Off Moves

Pick-off moves are often misunderstood; their primary purpose is to disrupt the timing of base runners and keep them close to their base. Every pitcher will pick runners off occasionally, however pitchers get into trouble when they try to be too fast and too tricky in their pursuit of getting free outs. Pitchers who pick off more often also throw balls away more often.

We want the minimum effective dose: pick off as little as possible to optimally discourage runners from stealing and getting large leads.

Lead Size

Righthanded pitchers have difficulty seeing first base while set and can only use peripheral vision to see over. Most righthanders won't be able to properly gauge the runner's lead size. If you're a righthander, your best bet is to use the other methods mentioned in this chapter to determine when to pick off.

I don't feel it's necessary to quantify lead size to determine when to throw over. I feel that a pitcher's experience and intuition will be the best guide in determining when a lead is too big and the runner must be chased back.

Additionally, the catcher should assist the pitcher in gauging lead size. Because the catcher has full sightlines to all bases, he can alert the pitcher with a sign, indicating that a pick-off attempt should be made.

Pick Off with Intent to Get an Out

It's useless to throw a soft, rainbow-arc throw to a base – it does nothing to put fear into a runner. All throws to bases should be made with intent to get an out. After all, if the pitcher does a good job of varying his delivery and holds, he is likely to catch the runner in a confused state. It's impossible to guess when a runner is ready to steal, so by throwing hard every time, you'll give yourself the chance to get the out on the rare occasion the runner is caught leaning. Pitchers kick themselves when they perform a lazy pick off move, only to see that the runner was, in fact, about to steal.

"Protecting Pitches"

Protecting ones pitches refers to "running counts" and the effect the ball-strike count has on a base runner's willingness to steal. Runners are most likely to succeed in stealing a base when they run on an offspeed pitch – a changeup, curve, slider, splitter, etc. These pitches have less velocity and thus take longer to reach the catcher. Additionally, offspeed pitches are more likely to be thrown down in the zone or in the dirt, making it all but impossible to throw out a fast runner. Smart runners steal on counts in which the pitcher is more likely to throw offspeed.

Offspeed & Breaking Ball Counts

Again, if a runner wants to steal, he will steal. But, the pitcher would prefer the runner to steal on a fastball so that the catcher is more likely to catch him. Counts in which a pitcher will throw fastballs more often than not are deemed fastball counts. These are typified by a pitcher who is behind or even in the count – he must catch up by throwing his most accurate pitch, typically the fastball. "Breaking ball counts," or "offspeed counts" are those where the pitcher is ahead and thus has room for error to attempt to get swings and misses.

Traditional "fastball counts:"

- 0-0
- 1-0
- 2-0
- 3-0
- 1-1
- 2-1
- 3-1
- 3-2

Traditional "breaking ball" or "offspeed counts:"

- 0-1
- 0-2
- 1-2
- 2-2

Note that these counts are generalizations, and all pitchers choose to throw their arsenal differently. The best base stealers watch pitchers intently to discern patterns for when they throw certain pitches, because it's impossible to fully predict what a pitcher will throw by count alone.

With an understanding of the counts on which runners generally choose to steal, the pitcher can protect himself by throwing over more often. If the pitcher intends to throw an 0-2 curveball, a predictable pitch, it makes sense to pick off one or more times to heavily discourage the runner from stealing.

Disrupting a Runner's Timing

The last key to holding runners is unpredictability. The jump refers to the base stealer's reaction time – how quickly he takes off once he sees the pitcher start his delivery to the plate. A good base stealer gets good jumps – he reacts quickly and optimizes every millisecond of the pitcher's delivery. If a runner gets a poor jump on a pitcher with a fast delivery, he will be out by a wide margin with even a poor throw from the catcher. When a pitcher changes his timing to the plate and effectively mixes in pick-off moves, he reduces the runner's ability to get a good jump.

Timing Disruptions – Holds

A pitcher must come set and pause for a minimum of one second before delivering a pitch. This does not apply to pick off attempts – he may pick off at any moment while time is live. Remember that base runners are in a tense position – a half squat ready to sprint – which takes a lot of muscular energy. Holding the ball for longer periods of time drains life from the legs of base runners and makes it unclear when the pitcher will deliver the ball.

Pitchers ineffective at holding runners fall into a pattern – they hold the ball for the same length of time on the vast majority of their pitches. Usually this is 1-2 seconds. All it takes to be a vastly more effective pitcher is to incorporate a wider range of holds before both pitching and picking off.

However, the two big players in hold varieties are the quick-pitch and the medium hold.

Hold Durations
1 Second – "Quick pitch"
2-3 Seconds – Medium hold
4-7 Seconds – Long hold

The quick pitch is effective after medium or long holds because the runner expects the pitcher to stay in a pattern of longer holds. Medium holds will make up the vast majority of a pitcher's mix, with long holds used sparingly. Long holds make the runner, hitter and umpire antsy – after the four second mark, both the hitter and umpire will consider calling time out (which is fine!). It's good to occasionally show the runner that a pitcher will hold for any length of time, even one so long that time gets called; this adds unpredictability. But, it's also important to keep the game moving along or the fielders will become bored and inattentive.

It's important to know that timing disruption negatively affects the hitter as well – he gets antsy and in a tense position, much like the runner. The pitcher will optimize his chances to get both the runner and hitter out when he mixes his holds effectively.

Timing Disruptions – Pick Offs

The goal is to ensure the runner is fearful that a pick-off attempt may occur at any moment. Because the pitcher can pick off without time restriction, it is ideal to mix pick-off attempts at all durations between 0-7 seconds. Once the runner has seen a pitcher pick off at all lengths of hold, he is forced to focus intently at all times, which slows reaction time.

Holds should deter most base runners from stealing as long as they have seen the pitcher try to pick off a teammate. For the fastest runners, however, more frequent pick-off attempts are necessary, in addition to mixing holds. The most brazen base runners require the most attention and pick-off attempts, but most pitchers will only pick off 5-10 times, on average, per 6-inning outing.

Examples of In-Game Disruption

Example #1 *(Bad)*: Fast runner on 1st base:

Pitch #1: Comes set, pauses 1 second, delivers pitch.
Pitch #2: Comes set, pauses 1.5 seconds, delivers pitch.
Pitch #3: Comes set, pauses 1 second, picks off to first base. (Runner is safe.)
Pitch #3: Comes set, pauses 1 second (runner takes off), delivers pitch.

The pitcher's mistake in the above example is that he does very little, aside from one pick-off attempt, to disrupt the runner's timing. The runner has figured out that the pitcher will go home in 1-1.5 seconds. So, knowing that the pitcher's pick-off attempt was not good enough to get him, he leans a little more to second base and counts to one second in his head. If the pitcher hasn't picked off in that time, he takes off with a great jump.

Example #2 *(Good)*: Fast runner on 1st base:

Pitch #1: Comes set, pauses 1 second, picks off to first base. (Runner is safe.)
Pitch #1: Comes set, pauses 3 seconds, delivers pitch.
Pitch #2: Comes set, pauses 3 seconds, picks off to first base. (Runner is safe.)
Pitch #2: Comes set, pauses 1 second (runner takes off), delivers pitch.

This pitcher has a good idea of how to hold runners – he both pitches and picks off with two different hold intervals. The runner can't get a good jump because the pitcher might pick off after one second or three seconds. So, the runner has to watch the pitcher more intently to ensure he doesn't leave too soon, just to have the pitcher pick him off.

Let's look at another example, one with a runner who is very fast and will be difficult to catch stealing:

Example #3 *(Good)*: Very fast runner on 1st base; crucial situation to keep runner off 2nd base.

Pitch #1: Comes set, pauses 1 second, picks off to first base. (Runner is safe.)
Pitch #1: Comes set, pauses 4 seconds, picks off to first base. (Runner is safe.)
Pitch #1: Comes set, pauses 3 seconds, delivers pitch.
Pitch #2: Picks off before coming set. (Runner is safe.)
Pitch #2: Comes set, pauses 5 seconds. Hitter asks for time out. Time is called.
Pitch #2: Comes set, pauses 1 second, delivers pitch.
Pitch #3: Comes set, pauses 3 seconds, picks off to first base. (Runner is safe.)
Pitch #3: Comes set, pauses 4 seconds (runner takes off), delivers pitch.

There's a lot going on there, but it represents heavy effort on the pitcher's part to keep the runner confused. The runner is forced to pay full attention to the pitcher, fearing a pick off at any length of hold. Additionally, long holds sap life from the runner's legs – staying in a tense, ready to run position takes a lot of energy and reduces reaction time. It's unlikely the runner will get a good jump in this situation, giving the catcher the best possible chance to catch him.

Let's now look at one more example, this one more complex – with pitch counts considered.

Example #4 *(Good)*: Fast runner on first base.

Pitch #1 (0-0): Comes set, pauses 3 seconds, delivers fastball. Ball 1.
Pitch #2 (1-0): Comes set, pauses 1 second, delivers fastball. Strike 1.

On pitch #2, the pitcher used a 1 second pause to welcome the runner to steal. Because the pitcher was throwing a fastball, being behind in the count, it's a bad pitch for the runner to steal on. So, the pitcher doesn't try too hard to discourage him because he is more likely to be thrown out.

Pitch #3 (1-1): Comes set, pauses 2 seconds, delivers fastball. Strike 2.
Pitch #4 (1-2): Comes set, pauses 0 seconds, picks off to first base. (Runner is safe.)
Pitch #4 (1-2): Comes set, pauses 4 seconds, delivers curveball. Foul.

On pitch #4, the pitcher picked off and then used a long hold to heavily discourage the runner from stealing. The pitcher was set to throw a curveball, so he made sure to protect his slower pitch by paying a bit more attention to the runner.

Pitch #5 (1-2) Comes set, pauses 2 seconds, picks off to first base. (Runner is safe.)
Pitch #5 (1-2): Comes set, pauses 1 second, delivers curveball. Strike 3.

This sequence was a good example of how a pitcher will protect his offspeed offerings from a steal by more heavily disrupting the runner. Yet, when the pitcher has decided to throw a fastball, he can be a little more lax, thus encouraging the runner to choose the fastball to attempt his steal. Remember – if a runner has decided to steal, all we can do is disrupt him and hope that he chooses a fastball. By picking off less before a fastball and more before an offspeed pitch, we can persuade the runner to choose a fastball for his steal attempt.

The Pitch Out

A pitch out is when a pitcher intentionally throws a ball into the unoccupied batter's box at chest height to give the catcher an easy pitch to throw out a runner. The pitch out is called only when the coach is convinced a runner will be attempting a steal.

Most pitch outs are called on the first pitch of an at-bat (0-0 count), and it's rare to ever see two pitch outs in a row, though they do happen. Coaches will only activate the pitch out if they are confident in the pitcher's ability to throw strikes, as he will immediately be behind in the count; this is the reason two are rarely used in the same at-bat. If a pitcher has been wild, and runner does not run on the pitch out, the coach has just put his pitcher closer to walking the hitter, which accomplishes the same goal as a stolen base.

Runners often fall into patterns just like pitchers, the most common being steal attempts on the first pitch of at-bats. If a runner has already attempted two steals in a game and gets on base a third time, a coach will often use an 0-0 pitch out to catch him right away. The pitch-out is also most frequently seen in situations where the base stealer is a very important run, such as when the score is close late in the game.

The pitcher will never call a pitch out himself; it's a coach-called play. However, a pitcher must be aware of the situation and properly execute the pitch – chest high, in the unoccupied batter's box, and thrown hard. Soft-tossing the pitch out defeats the purpose because slower pitches give the runner extra steps toward the base.

FAQ – *You claim that stepping off isn't effective against base stealers. When is it appropriate?*

Stepping off has a purpose – resetting the pitcher, the fielders and the hitter.

If a hitter has fouled off a few pitches in a row, a pitcher might come set, hold, and then step off or pick off. This will disrupt the hitter's timing.

Additionally, if a fielder is out of position or just made a long, tiring run for a ball, the pitcher might give him a chance to catch his breath by stepping off. Fielders appreciate this.

Lastly, the game does not start until the pitcher is 100% ready. Wind blows, dirt gets kicked around, contact lenses get dry, uniforms come untucked, cleats get snagged, and the sun often burns the eyes – all are reasons to step off, reset oneself and then return to the mound ready to pitch. A pitcher should never throw a pitch when he is uncomfortable – that discomfort may be the reason he loses focus, leaves a pitch down the middle and gives up a game-changing home run. Step off, refocus, and return when ready; everyone else will wait.

FAQ – *The head is the only body part that can move once set. Can a pitcher use the head to his advantage over the runner?*

Yes. Good base stealers will watch a pitcher's head as a window to his intentions. Pitchers, when thinking about the runner, will look the runner's way. When the pitcher forgets about the runner or turns his attention to the plate and/or his pitch, he will look to the plate.

While the previous two points are somewhat obvious, they're important to remember because they can be manipulated to the pitcher's advantage. Many pitchers will fall into the pattern of looking at the runner only when they're concerned about him, and then look back at the plate when ready to pitch.

The runner can easily pick up on this, and will decide to take off to the next base as soon as the head turns back to the plate. A deceptive pitcher will mix up his head movements, attempting the "head fake" seen in football and basketball. Lefthanders especially can become skilled at lifting their leg while looking at the runner, and all pitchers can stare down runners on second base. Lefthanders will want to vary their head movements as much as possible, so the runner feels fear regardless of whether the pitcher is looking at him. Righthanders will not have quite the advantage with runners on first, but nonetheless should vary the amount of times they rubberneck toward the runner and make eye contact where applicable.

CHAPTER 5

PITCHING MECHANIC MAXIMS

Consistent pitching mechanics provide the pitcher with maximum velocity and location consistency via effective energy transfer and reliable release point. Pitchers who learn to stride directly to their target, shift their weight at the proper moment and keep their head, shoulders and chest tracking to the plate throw the most strikes with the most velocity and the least amount of arm stress. Good pitching mechanics are the foundation for a long, healthy career in baseball.

Brevity is my goal when discussing pitching mechanics, so I will not delve into the thousands of ways a person can deliver a baseball. Because chapters 1 & 2 discussed the windup and stretch mechanics, this chapter will cover the hand break, stride and beyond. Each topic will be dissected into maxims – the major action points in the delivery that must be achieved by every pitcher, regardless of body size, shape, age, skill level, etc.

This chapter is unique in that I have two explanations for each maxim. I will have a long explanation for those readers who want every detail of why I teach what I teach. Each topic, however, will be introduced with an abstract – a concise explanation of the core concept. After the abstract, proceed for the long explanation, or simply skip ahead to the drills and fixes for each mechanical flaw.

Pro Pitching Maxims
1. 2-D Hand Break
2. Optimal Stride Length
3. Perpendicular Landing
4. Level Shoulders and 90° Elbow
5. Glove Tuck
6. Backside Triple Extension
7. Forward Chest Drive
8. Upright Head
9. Late Elbow Quadruple Extension

The list above is not an exhaustive one of "what good pitchers do." Rather, it's a list of good positions that, if achieved, will necessitate the achievement of one or more additional advantageous body positions. I could discuss much more about the pitching motion, but these instructions will be more practical if we keep things simple.

Maxim #1: Two-Dimensional Hand Break ——————————

Abstract: The hands should break smoothly down, back and up until the upper arm is level with or slightly below the shoulders when the lead foot lands. Length of arm swing is individually variable and does not determine throwing velocity. 2-D refers to preventing the arm from wrapping behind the back. While a 2-D arm swing is ideal, the arm may wrap around the back without negative effect as long as it aligns with the body by time the lead foot strikes.

2-D Hand Break: Full Explanation

The hand break is relatively simple; suffice it to say that staying in one plane (what I refer to as two-dimensions) simplifies everything that comes later in the delivery. Wrapping the hand way behind the back, digging the hand down toward the dirt, and locking the arm out as the hand reaches all complicate the timing of the arm swing. The upper arm must be close to shoulder height at foot strike; reaching excessively behind the body will increase the likelihood that the arm will drag behind the body as the torso accelerates toward the plate.

What We Don't Want

Creating a 2-D Hand Break

I've found that showing the ball to the first baseman (lefthanders) or third baseman (righthanders) will help improve arm swing timing and prevent wrapping. Showing the ball requires the fingers to stay vertical, pointing to the sky. When in this vertical showing position, it's impossible to push the hand behind the body – the only way it will work is if the hand and fingers point downward. So, if the ball is up and visible, the arm must be traveling in 2-D - problem solved! But, because the arm swing is very much an innate quality, it will take a tremendous amount of repetition to make positive change. Fortunately, these drills are very easy and quickly replicated.

The drill for re-training the hand break to stay in one plane is simple: back up to a wall, and practice the hand break and arm swing. The wall will serve as a barrier to prevent the arm from wrapping behind the back, giving immediate feedback (don't bump the wall). Use the vertical hand position while performing this drill for maximum effect.

Maxim # 2: Optimal Stride Length

Abstract: Longer strides correlate with higher throwing velocities. Increasing stride length has a positive effect on velocity via improved weight transfer, low-back energy re lease, leg muscle recruitment, linear momentum and torso angle. An overly long stride, however, can have a negative, braking effect and drastically decrease downward pitch trajectory. A focus on hip flexibility and strong leg muscle recruitment should be enough to achieve optimal stride length with little conscious effort.

The Stride – Full Explanation

Average stride length is 80% of a pitcher's height. In my academy, I find that stride length correlates with a pitcher's velocity. However, there are always exceptions and not every pitcher needs an exceptional stride to throw exceptionally hard. I believe that pitchers who stride closer to 100% or more of their height will maximize transfer of their body's energy and subsequently reach more of their potential velocity ceiling.

An appeal to reason will support this: Infielders and catchers make throws on the run and from a standstill, stifling stride length. Catchers can throw well into the 70s from their knees; shortstops can throw balls into the 80s with just a short crow hop after fielding a slow roller. These players don't throw maximally with these short or nonexistent strides, but they do throw at a high percentage of their max. There is tremendous variability in arm strength, the genetic predisposition in muscular strength and elasticity in the arm, which accounts for much of why some players throw faster than others.

But, with all other factors being equal, a group of pitchers with longer strides will throw harder, on average, than a group with shorter strides. This relates to power transfer, use of the legs, creating advantageous body angles, creating and transferring stored energy in the lower back, and developing linear momentum down the mound.

Power Transfer

When the stride leg is lifted, all body weight shifts to the drive leg. This weight must be effectively transferred down the mound and into the baseball. The hips will start the motion down the mound by peeking out, starting a passive descent as weight is shifted forward. A longer stride allows this momentum to build over a longer period of time, which should make a higher power output easier to control. A short stride with powerful weight shift makes for a chaotic power transfer at release, which will decrease a pitcher's consistency and accuracy. Additionally, the pitcher must have the leg strength required to brace his front knee at a slight bend (140-150 degrees), which transfers power from his legs to his torso. If the momentum forces the stride leg to continue bending once the foot has planted, energy will dissipate in the legs and velocity will decrease.

Leg Recruitment & Linear Momentum

The pitcher's only chance to use his legs – the powerful motors driving the lower body – is when he strides. A long stride allows the legs to work freely, extending hard to propel the body down the mound. At longer stride lengths, much more of the posterior chain (the glutes, hamstring and lower back) is recruited and activated to transfer energy. A short stride does not allow the legs to effectively shift weight or reach full contractile range of motion. I believe that a slight push by the legs, which is made more effective at a longer stride, helps transfer the last little bit of energy. When the pitcher is at nearly full stride, the more powerfully he can shift his weight, the more energy will be explosively applied to the pitch. Strong leg recruitment aids the late energy transfer that will most positively impact pitch velocity.

Increased Lower Back Energy Release

The upper body wants to stay tall during the stride to maintain proper weight shift. To do this, the lower back must hyperextend. The farther the pitcher strides, the more his lower back must hyperextend to maintain a vertical torso. Hyperextending the lower back stores energy that is powerfully released when the torso pushes forward just before release of the pitch. The greater the stride, the more the lower back will contribute to increase a pitcher's velocity.

Creating a Low Torso Angle

A low torso angle, ideally around 45°, is ideal for the pitcher to create higher velocities. The most common flaw I find in slow-throwing pitchers is a high torso angle. If a pitcher exhibits a long stride, adequate flexibility and good weight transfer, he will push his torso down the mound toward the plate. This, coupled with a long stride, will create a lower relative body angle. Releasing pitches from a lower torso angle will allow the torso to supply more momentum to the arm, which will in turn require less muscular energy from the arm itself. The arm can then accelerate farther in front of the body, which is an advantageous position where leverages are considered.

Perceived Velocity

When a pitcher strides longer he releases his pitch closer to the plate. This requires the hitter to react faster, thus making the pitch more difficult to hit. "Perceived" velocity from factors such as stride length are important in maximizing the effectiveness and deception offered by a pitcher.

Pitch Trajectory

Though everyone in the baseball industry recognizes the virtues of a long stride, it is important to consider one contrary effect – a lower release height and decreased downward trajectory. As a quick experiment, stand up from your chair. Widen your stance until you're in the widest split position you can muster. How much shorter are you now versus when standing with feet together? A foot? More?

The downward trajectory of a pitch is important – steeper downhill angles are vastly more difficult to lift into the air for extra base hits. Breaking balls also become sharper when released with a steeper downhill trajectory. By striding exceptionally far, a pitcher sacrifices his pitch angle. This does not mean that we should aim to stride short; it just means over-striding is not optimal, either. We need to find the balance – an optimal stride.

Braking Effect

While a longer stride will usually provide more power to ones mechanics, over-striding will have the opposite effect. If a pitcher strides too far, he will be unable to transfer energy over the lead foot, resulting in diminished velocity via a braking effect. Think back to standing in the split position a moment ago: It was a "no man's land" regarding weight shift – equal weight displacement makes it difficult to move the body in either direction.

Inadequate Strength

It is important to recognize the role of the core and hips in the stride. The core and hips control the body as it glides forward. As the pitcher strides out, he is essentially in midair, which requires tremendous core and hip strength to maintain proper body position. Weak athletes have a difficult time controlling their bodies, and a longer period in the air (via a lengthened stride) will be difficult for them to control. General core and bodily weakness is often one reason athletes settle into a short stride.

<u>Pros & Cons of Increasing Stride Length</u>

PRO:	CON:
1. More explosive weight shift	1. Reduced downward pitch trajectory
2. Better backside recruitment	2. Possible braking effect
3. Increased low back energy storage and release	3. Weak pitchers have difficulty controlling body
4. Increased perceived velocity	
5. Lower Torso Angle	

Creating the "Optimal" Stride

Optimal stride length is that which maximizes a pitcher's weight transfer and downhill angle. I do not find it useful to teach any specific stride length. I feel that each pitcher's natural stride length will reveal itself when the following conditions are met:

1. Hips are flexible enough to not be a limiting factor
2. Weight transfer is late and powerful
3. Core and hip strength is adequate to control the body while midair

The only time I will actively tell my students to stride farther is when I catch them being lazy, throwing without full body recruitment. This usually means the legs aren't pushing the athlete down the mound; rather, the leg is being lifted and simply placed back down.

I do not prescribe striding drills to find optimal stride length. If a pitcher has an exceptionally short stride that appears to be holding him back, I will ask him to lift his leg faster and push himself down the mound slightly harder. This conscious addition of speed to both the leg lift and leg push will give him extra linear momentum and will propel him farther down the mound.

What to Do

If a pitcher has a short stride and is inflexible and weak, striding drills are likely to be a waste of time – his physical makeup is inhibiting skill development. Conversely, if a pitcher is strong and flexible, increasing stride length will be as simple as increasing the speed and intensity of the delivery.

If a pitcher feels his stride is too short, or simply wants to experiment with lengthening his stride:

1. Institute daily hip stretching and strengthening exercises. Strengthening is beyond the scope of this book, but a few of my favorite exercises and stretches are included below.
2. Increase the speed of the delivery – a faster leg lift and slightly harder push on the rubber will provide an immediate increase in stride length (provided flexibility is not limiting the athlete).
3. Institute a quality strength & conditioning program. Increasing core, leg and hip strength will allow the pitcher to better control his body at higher velocities and while midair in the stride.

The Most Effective Hip Flexibility Drills

Lateral Hips:

1. The Sumo Squat	2. Elevated Half-Kneel	3. Elevated Adductor

Anterior/Posterior Hips:

1. Elevated Hip Flexor	2. Quad Lunge	3. Hamstring Kickback

The Most Effective Hip Strengthening Drills

1. Mini-Band Goblet Squat	2. Mini-Band Side Shuffle	3. Mini-Band Monster Walk

Maxim #3: Perpendicular Landing

Abstract: An ideal stride landing is perpendicular from the ankle of the drive foot to the center of the plate. Striding too far open reduces velocity via reduced hip and core recruitment. Striding too far closed puts additional stress on the arm and hips while making it difficult to throw sharp breaking balls and command the gloveside of the plate. Striding off center also misdirects a pitcher's energy, causing unnecessary rotation that makes it difficult to throw strikes at peak velocity.

Perpendicular Landing – Full Explanation

When I say perpendicular, I mean intersecting with the front facet of the plate at a 90° angle. When a pitcher lands, he will strike the mound with his heel. Contrary to conventional wisdom that pitchers should point their toe downward during the leg lift, I find that it's irrelevant – nearly all pitchers, hard throwing or otherwise, land on their heels because of the downward slope of the mound. The heel will almost always strike first, so we do not need to worry about the toe-point during leg lift, and can thus focus only on landing in proper body position. I also hypothesize that a heel-first landing is beneficial, as it allows the stride leg to extend and transfer energy into torso flexion. The weight shift from heel to toe is preferable over landing directly on the toe, which can cause a braking effect in the weight shift.

I also don't worry too much about what a pitcher does before landing – all of the pre-landing motion is somewhat irrelevant; what matters is how the pitcher lands. Many pitchers, Felix Hernandez and Jared Weaver among them, turn their torsos significantly away from the plate while in their leg lift. This is not problematic because both of these pitchers "unwind" and land straight to the plate. While keeping the body perpendicular during the leg lift is much easier, it is not necessary – landing perpendicular is the maxim we must achieve, and as long as it is accomplished, we can allow for variability in what precedes it. Many successful pitchers do many different things before landing. But, they all land perpendicular plus/minus a few degrees. However, it is much more difficult for young pitchers to undo a significant wrapping motion, so I teach my amateurs to stay as perpendicular to their targets as possible. Look at the photo below on the left – see how far off line the lead foot is? It will be very difficult to land straight.

Pointing the stride leg directly toward the center of the plate is necessary for all pitchers because it aligns the body with the plate and ensures 90° of trunk rotation toward the plate. A common flaw I see is the chest showing to the plate too early or striding too far to the gloveside (commonly known as "flying open"). Those who fly open lose the ability to rotate fully in both the hips and torso. Conversely, those who land too far closed (known as landing across the body), either with their stride or trunk rotation, have difficulty pitching to the gloveside of the plate and getting on top of a breaking ball. Pitchers who land too far closed must rotate farther to force the ball to the middle of the plate. This causes the arm to straighten earlier, resulting in increased stress and decreased velocity.

Additionally, landing too far open or closed misdirects a pitcher's energy – I want the pitcher's momentum driving directly to the center of the plate; any deviation from this will force the pitcher to compensate by becoming overly rotational, which is a negative (addressed later in this chapter). It will also negatively affect the follow through position of the pitcher, causing him to fall off the mound one way or another. This, in turn, has an adverse effect on the pitcher's fielding ability.

Chest Closed — Chest Open
Stride Closed — Stride Open

I see six flaws in pitchers who do not stride optimally. I will break down my solutions to these flaws according to landing position – open or closed.

Lands overly closed:
1. Stride direction is angled toward the arm side at landing
2. Torso (but not stride direction) cannot open adequately at landing
3. Both stride direction and torso are too far closed at landing

Lands open:
1. Stride direction is angled toward the glove side at landing
2. Torso (but not stride direction) rotates open too soon at landing
3. Both stride direction and torso are too far open at landing

The Perfect Landing

At the point of landing, the upper arm of both the glove and pitching arms should be in line with the shoulders. The pitcher should be staring down his front shoulder out of the corner of his eye.

Creating the Perfect Perpendicular Landing

My process in cleaning up a stride is first done by simple coaching. It's important to realize that many pitchers won't know the flaws in their deliveries. So, it's unfair to assume they can't do something until they are asked to do it. I won't overcomplicate things by instituting drills when a simple verbal cue and call to focus will do the job.

1. Show the pitcher his stride via photo, video, or asking him to freeze after a throw
2. Draw a line toward the plate and ask the pitcher to stride onto it. Chalk and tape work great.
3. If the pitcher can do it, no further coaching is needed – he simply needs to focus on doing it on every pitch.
4. If the pitcher cannot do it, further diagnosis is needed.

Further Diagnosis & Coaching: Pitcher Who Lands Too Closed

I use four possible fixes for this, and all are aimed at redirecting the pitcher's torso toward the center of the plate. They are listed in order of simplicity, so attempt to fix the problem in order. If the first fix works, stop there. If not, use the first fix and add additional fixes until the problem is solved.

1. Ankle Toward the Plate

This is the number one cue to fix a closed stride. By emphasizing pointing his ankle at his target, the pitcher will direct his lower body toward the center of the plate rather than out into the arm-side batter's box.

2. Tuck the Elbow; Two Eyes to the Plate

First Cue: Tuck the Elbow

Pulling the glove elbow in tightly to the side will activate muscles on the gloveside, which will pull the torso slightly back toward perpendicular. This cue works better from the stretch than it does from the windup, but still works for both.

Glove elbow moves away from midline.

Second Cue: Two Eyes

Looking to the plate from the corner of the eye is good, unless it causes the pitcher to close off too much. Pitchers who land too closed must force their chest a bit more toward the plate. The chest follows the eyes; if we get both eyes on the plate, the body will typically rotate 10-20° toward perpendicular. This is a very effective cue from the windup.

3. Offset the Stance

If the pitcher naturally steps across his body, we can simply account for this natural action and offset it while in the stretch position. The behavior stays the same, but by starting in a different position, the result is changed. This fix works only while in the stretch.

Normal Stance

Open Stance

4. Stretch the Hips

The above three fixes will work. However, it is important to address what may be an underlying physical problem – tight hips. Pitchers with a deficit in hip rotation or with tight hip flexors and IT bands will find it difficult to land in a perpendicular stride. The following stretches will make achieving an ideal stride much easier.

1. Quad Lunge

2. Wall IT Band

3. Knee-Knee

4. Hurdler Stretch

5. Elevated Adductor

6. Seated Hip Opener

Further Diagnosis & Coaching: Pitcher Who Lands Open

I use five possible fixes for those who land too far open. They are listed in order of simplicity, so attempt to fix the problem in order. If the first fix works, stop there. If not, use the first fix and add additional fixes until the problem is solved.

1. Ankle Toward the Plate

This cue works equally well for those who stride too far open.

2. Glue Chin to Shoulder; Corner of Eye to Plate

The chest follows the eyes. By looking at the plate via the corner of the eye, the pitcher will tend not to rotate toward the plate. The pitcher should always use his glove arm as his sightline to the plate. By tucking the chin down to the head of the shoulder and keeping the shoulder up, he will force his chest to connect with both his shoulder and his sightline. If the chin stays put and the body wants to fly open, the head will off the target, thus alerting the pitcher that he flew open too soon. If chin stays locked on the shoulder and eyes to the plate, the pitcher is almost assured of staying perpendicular to his target.

3. Reach Glove Hand Across Body; Point Shoulder Blade

Flying open is typified by the glove arm dumping out and down toward the gloveside. To counteract this, I will often have the pitcher overcompensate by pointing his glove arm across his body and showing his shoulder blade to the plate. Then, if he still flies open later, his flying open will bring him back to perpendicular rather than open due to the overcompensation. This is the same principle as offsetting the stance. If the pitcher tends to open up 20° too soon, have him point his arm 20° across his body.

4. Offset the Stance

We can close the pitcher's stance the same way we open the stance for those who land across their body.

Normal Stance   Closed Stance

5. Stretch the Hips

1. Quad Lunge   2. Wall IT Band

3. Knee-Knee

Maxim #4: Level Shoulders and 90° Elbow

Abstract: As the striding pitcher lands, the shoulders and upper arms must stay level or tilted slightly upward, and the throwing elbow should be at or very near 90°. This ensures that the torso will stay upright, forcing the lower back to store energy that will later contribute to pitch velocity. High shoulders keep the weight shifted back until it is forced to come forward as the hips begin to rotate. Low shoulders indicate an improper weight shift that will decrease both velocity and accuracy.

Level Shoulders – Full Explanation

Keeping level shoulders forces the pitcher to do things we want: keep his weight back and keep his eyes tracking to his target. Because the mound is sloped, the pitcher must resist the downward angle by keeping more of his weight on his back leg. If the shoulders slope downward, matching the slope of the mound, the weight shifts too early, resulting in a major loss of power and nearly all pitches going downward into the dirt.

Leveling the Shoulders

Fortunately, this is one of the easier mechanical maxims to fix and requires little drilling. Typically, all we need to do is refer to a pitcher's shoulders and weight shift to gain compliance.

Shoulder cues: 1. "Shoulders tall"
                  2. "Shoulders level"
                  3. "Shoulders high"

Weight shift cues: 1. "Keep the weight back"
                      2. "Sit on the back leg longer"
                      3. "Stay on the back leg as long as possible"
                      4. "Push the lead hip out slightly

Again, I find that pitchers who struggle with this quickly find success with my verbal cues. But, when troubles persist, two simple drills help remedy the problem:

Drill 1: Dry Landing

Incredibly simple: Have the pitcher start his delivery, without a ball, and pause once he strides to his landing position. Where are his shoulders? If too low, show him, and have him repeat until he can get it right. Again – this problem does not require a complex solution.

Drill 2: Hip Bump

For the few pitchers who really don't get the feeling of keeping the weight back, the hip bump drill will work. It only requires a bucket, wall, or other stationary object. In the graphic below, I used a bucket.

Have the pitcher start from the stretch and lift his leg. At the top of his leg lift, make him touch his foot to the bucket. Then, have him fall toward the plate, keeping his foot in contact with the bucket as long as possible. His hips will shift forward while his weight stays back, giving him the feel of a somewhat extreme but proper weight shift.

Drill 3: Long Toss

Long toss, which involves throwing at an upward angle, helps the pitcher learn to load his back hip and keep weight back longer, which prevents the shoulders from tilting forward too soon. It is impossible to throw at a high trajectory with level or downward-sloping shoulders. To help pitchers learn the leg mechanics of shifting weight and keeping their shoulders level, a simple game of long toss will help dramatically.

90° Elbow

Landing with the elbow up at a right angle is crucial to ensuring proper timing in the pitching sequence. From the 90° position, the hips turn and the arm lays back. If the elbow is at a different angle or the forearm is lagging behind and not yet vertical, the pitcher will struggle to get on top of his pitches. This leads to inconsistent downhill angle, inconsistent spin, poor breaking ball sharpness and depth, and inconsistent accuracy. I simply suggest drilling hand breaks to the landing position and making phantom throws to reinforce the 90° arm angle.

Maxim #5: Glove Tuck

Abstract: The glove tuck serves to increase recruitment of the core musculature on the gloveside, which helps to accelerate the forward rotation of the hips and core. Keeping the glove arm closer to the center of mass also prevents misdirection of energy, increasing velocity and accuracy while improving a pitcher's fielding position after follow through. The glove does not actually travel back toward the body during a pitch. Rather, the body travels toward the glove. But, I have found that practicing pulling in tightly enhances the feel of the drill.

Glove Tuck –Full Explanation

We need the glove to tuck for a few reasons, all of which lead to increased consistency and forward power transfer. At the core of this is muscle recruitment on the gloveside of the body.

The Lats and Obliques

When the glove arm stays tucked in tightly, the latissimus dorsi – the largest and most influential muscle of the back – is strongly activated. Additionally, because the body lands perpendicular to the plate, the obliques, the lateral muscles of the core, are responsible for much of the rotational crunch toward the plate. Pulling in the glove arm helps laterally compress the core, which increases oblique activation. By increasing both lat and oblique activation, the body will more strongly drive toward the plate, which will improve the torso angle and push the release point further toward the plate; this increases both actual and perceived velocity.

Compact Body Position

Good (compact) Glove Tuck   Bad (loose) Glove Tuck

If we are going to create and maintain a precise, repeatable release point window, we must be as compact as possible. By compact, I simply mean keeping the limbs and energy as central to the center of mass as we can. Arms are long – if they're flailing they will pull the body off-center and affect the pitcher's balance and direction – all of which will negatively influence the pitch. By yanking the glove in tightly to the body, we eliminate the possibility of the glove arm pulling our body off its track toward the target.

Reciprocal Action

The core and hips are reciprocal in that when one side contracts to rotate, the other side of the body must follow. So, when the glove arm strongly tucks, the muscle activation of the gloveside of the body will help propel the armside toward the strike zone. In this way, the gloveside of the body has a positive effect on the speed of the throwing arm.

Hip and Backside Triple Extension

By activating the glove side of the body, the hips on that side will rotate strongly to assist in pulling the body toward the target. The further the torso moves toward the plate, the more the backside of the body must extend, which creates a solid base and foundation for the pitcher to transfer his momentum. Triple extension is explained as maxim #6.

Committing to the Glove Tuck

The glove tuck requires an incredibly high number of repetitions to "stick." The drill I prescribe is simple, and the concept itself is basic. But, pitchers who fail to tuck their glove have likely been failing to do so as long as they have pitched, and so the habit runs deep. This drill absolutely will not work, and a good glove tuck will not be developed, without months of focused attention to properly tucking the glove on every throw. Pitchers have to truly believe in the change if they're to make it work; those who are only half-committed are unlikely to change.

Wall Glove-Tuck Drill (a lifelong drill)

Because we want the glove tuck to be tight and compact, using a wall is ideal to train compliance. Simply have the pitcher line up parallel with a wall with roughly 6 to 8 inches clearance. He should then raise his arms into perpendicular landing position, and finally pull his glove in as hard as possible while pivoting on the back foot. The wall helps to prevent the pitcher from spinning too much and reinforces forward body movement.

Maxim #6: Backside Triple Extension

Abstract: Triple extension refers to the achievement of full extension of the joints of the hip, knee and ankle, which pushes the body forward with optimal force, creating a low torso angle. An optimal stride, powerful hip rotation and strong glute and ham string musculature all contribute to triple extension. Those without triple extension typically exhibit an improper weight shift and inflexible hips.

Backside Triple Extension – Full Explanation

As the pitcher strides forward to his target, the back leg straightens to allow the stride to reach full distance. The back leg is typically straight or nearly straight when the pitcher lands; from this position the hips and core should start to rotate and push the upper body toward the plate. When the drive hip, drive knee and drive ankle fully extend, I call this triple extension.

Triple extension is crucial for giving the pitcher a full base of support from which he can transfer energy toward the plate. What I commonly see with amateur pitchers, though, is a back leg with poor extension at the hip, bending severely at the knee, and lifting off the ground at or before release of the pitch. This is not what we want because the lift-off of the drive leg causes a braking effect on the upper body, an upright torso angle, poor chest extension toward the plate and decreased velocity.

Examples of a poor back leg (little to no extension)

Examples of a strong backside achieving triple extension

As the arm accelerates, the back leg must remain straight as the hips pivot. The rotation of the pitcher around his lead hip transfers rotational energy to the drive leg. Then, as rotational energy transmits to the backside, the drive foot will also pivot and rotate outward until it lifts off the ground. The drive leg will kick high up into the air while rotating, finally landing beside the pitcher.

The Overly-Linear Flaw

Pitchers have varying degrees of triple extension, and we don't necessarily need a locked back leg. But, I view the mechanics as flawed and needing change if the back foot lifts off the ground and if the back knee bends to an angle sharper than 150°. If either flaw is present, the pitcher is losing power and must increase his backside extension. I call these pitchers overly-linear, in that their drive leg shoots forward toward the catcher rather than pivoting and rotating with the hips.

I struggle to understand the mechanism behind the drive leg lifting and driving forward. All pitchers' drive legs straighten during the stride. But, why some pitchers' legs bend and shoot forward rather than staying straight and pivoting (a much simpler bodily solution), is baffling. I have addressed glute weakness, hip weakness and hip inflexibility and have yet to find any strong correlations. I also look at the weight shift, and have found that a later weight shift has a positive effect – pitchers who tend to jump too hard toward the plate often have poor triple extension. But, what I unequivocally do know is that helping to train the hips to pivot upon foot strike increases compliance greatly with triple extension.

Teaching Backside Triple Extension

Feel Drill: Wall Push Drill

The pitcher should lean into a wall with most of his weight pushing forward. He should then pivot hard on the back foot like squishing a bug…a really big, mean bug. This drill helps to teach the body to activate the muscles in the lateral hips, glutes and hamstrings, all of which help triple-extend the drive leg.

Feel Drill: Foot Flick Drill

The student should set up in a wide landing stance and lean forward. Then, the focus is on flicking the ball of the foot backward, as if kicking sand up and backward with the foot. The foot will rotate, taking off into the air. A bucket or chair is a great aid to give the pitcher a target height over which he needs to flick his back leg.

Lifelong Drill: Rocker Drill with Foot Down (with or without towel or club)

The rocker drill is a lifelong drill and can be used with or without a ball. It's the ideal position to begin ones warm up during a throwing session. A towel or indian club can be held in the hand as an object to reach out with. Striking a target with the towel (not the club!) can help challenge the student to reach further over his front side. I like using indian clubs, as they will exploit over-rotation and reinforce moving straight to the target.

Start as wide as is comfortable, about 75% of stride length. The pitcher will rock forward, rock back, and finally rock forward again while forcefully pivoting the back foot in the squishing/flicking motion. The best way to ensure triple extension compliance is to simply keep the back foot firm to the ground throughout the entire throw and follow-through.

Lifelong Drill: Rocker Drill with Foot Flick

The foot flick rocker drill is a progression in which the foot stays no longer stays planted. When we allow the pitcher to start kicking up and around with his back foot, he's going to start bringing his knee forward, like he always has. This drill must be monitored in the mirror or by a coach to ensure the pitcher isn't reverting to old habits of poor triple extension once he's allowed to let his foot come off the ground. Foot on the ground = forced compliance. Foot in the air = compliance only if strong focus is employed. Progress to this drill only if triple extension is starting to feel like second nature.

Beneficial Stretches

A lack of hip flexor flexibility and overall hip mobility will negatively affect a pitcher's ability to achieve triple extension. I recommend performing the same stretches as outlined for creating optimal stride length.

Throwing Recommendations

For those who struggle with backside triple extension, it's best to force the back foot to stay in contact with the ground when throwing. This can be accomplished by simply throwing from the rocker position or full mechanics while keeping the back foot down the entire time. The pitcher's backside triple extension will improve as long as the pitcher resists the urge to lift the back foot and let it travel forward.

Maxim #7: Forward Chest Drive ——————————

Abstract: The pitcher is forced to rotate toward the plate; the chest must finish square to the plate. As such, the focus should not be on rotating, because rotation must happen anyway. Rather, the pitcher should force his chest and torso directly forward to the plate to build late, forceful extension, which, when coupled with torso rotation, will yield maximum pitch velocity.

Chest Forward – Full explanation

A common misconception is that the pitcher must rotate toward the plate. While rotation must happen for the pitcher to bring his torso from perpendicular to parallel with the plate, this 90° rotation will happen naturally. Because this minimum rotation happens naturally, the pitcher should never attempt to rotate farther or faster. When pitchers think about rotating toward the plate, they create an indirect path toward their target and this detracts from forward extension, consistency and proper hand position.

The chest is the key to a perfect set of powerful mechanics. The chest signifies the center of mass in the upper body, and it's the point we want to drive toward the target. When the chest pushes forward, rotation in the torso will happen on its own. The chest push will improve backside triple extension and torso angle while helping to release stored energy in the lower back. As the torso accelerates faster, with more extension toward the plate, so must the arm. This not only has a positive effect on velocity, but release point and hand position as well. In Chapter 9 I discuss in depth the role of the chest in pitch accuracy and target alignment.

The center of the chest should always drive straight toward the target

Forward Extension and Velocity

When the pitcher lands from his stride, we want the arm to take a direct path to the target. This is easily accomplished by forcing the upper body directly to the target, and the center point of the upper body is the chest. When the chest aligns with the target, so must the hand – then, as the arm accelerates, it does so in a direct line with the catcher's mitt.

I have found through tremendous amounts of trial and error with radar gun feedback that the pitcher always throws hardest when he gets the most extension. When the pitcher thinks "out" to his target – moving toward it rather than rotating to it or pulling his arm down – his body will force more of its available internal rotation and torso energy in a direct path. If we want to reach maximum velocity, we can't have any energy "leaking" from the mechanics – a direct path has the least leaks.

Release Point and Hand Position

Once the pitcher's lead foot strikes, the upper arm should be parallel with the ground and the forearm in the vertical position, or very close to it. From this point we want the fingers to stay behind the ball so they apply as much of their force as possible through the center. Pitch flight and force application is discussed at length in the preface to chapters 6, 7 and 8.

When a pitcher rotates to his target rather than pushing forward with his chest, the extra rotation affects the torso, then the arm, and finally the hand. The final effect on the hand is a slight supination – the hand rolls to the side and slightly underneath the ball. This slight side roll will make a fastball and changeup cut and a curveball or slider sweep across the zone in a loopy, soft-breaking fashion.

Poor finger position as a result of excessive trunk rotation (hand slips to side of ball) Good finger position as a result of forward chest drive

As will be discussed in chapters 6, 7 and 8, we want our fingers above the ball on all pitches. Over-rotation causes hand and finger position error due to the effect of centrifugal force accelerating the arm in a circular path. This causes the fingers to slip beneath or beside the ball, leading to unwanted cut, decreased velocity and softer break. Pushing the chest forward upon foot strike will keep the pitcher's hand above the ball, allowing him to have both a consistent release point and finger position as acceleration of the arm begins.

Teaching the Forward Chest

Verbal Cues: 1. "Crunch your abs forward and down"
2. "Chest forward"
3. "Reach and push the chest"

It's important to demonstrate a feeling of forward core activation – those who over-rotate activate their obliques much more than their abdominals, and so we want to get them to feel what it's like to crunch forward to the target. Asking the pitcher to squeeze his abs together to draw his ribcage down and forward will help him understand how this feels.

Feel Drill: Band-Assisted Crunch

The pitcher should get in landing position with a band held overhead. He should then push his chest forward maintaining long arms. The added resistance of the band will force the pitcher to engage his core and push hard to reach outward as far as possible.

Feel Drill: Medicine Ball Soccer Throw

Throwing a medicine ball soccer style will reinforce a strong forward chest push and core crunch. One could add a rotational component to make this throw more similar to the baseball pitch, but I choose to keep it anterior only in nature. Because rotation will naturally happen while throwing, we don't need to reinforce it during drills, especially when the goal is to break the student of his over-rotation habit.

Lifelong Drill: Towel Drill

The towel drill is a classic drill that most pitchers have done at some point in their careers. I like to use a short, thick, rolled towel – about 12 inches in length at most. Long towels tend to flop around in the hand, negatively affecting hand position and the realistic feel of the arm swing. To perform, all the pitcher needs to do is start in rocker position and push his chest forward and "throw" (without letting go) to strike a target as far forward as possible. The hand must strike slightly downward on a target, ensuring that hand position is above the pitch and the pitcher isn't swooping around the ball.

Lifelong Drill: Indian Club Rocker Drill

I love indian clubs because they exploit over-rotation in the delivery. Because they are heavy and extend arm length by about 15 inches, it's immediately apparent when the elbow flies out rather than driving straight to the target. All one has to do is swing the club in the same manner he would throw, scooping back up to the start position during follow-through. This drill should NOT be done violently! Go very gently and the let club swing you, not vice-versa.

Throwing Recommendations

The chest forward cue is a simple one that, in most instances, requires only verbal reminders to boost compliance. Pitchers need only throw with a constant mind on pushing toward their target, not rotating. Keeping the head upright helps, as does focus on crunching the core forward. Instruction to feel the abdominals contract to draw the ribcage down and forward will keep a pitcher on track.

Maxim #8: Upright Head

Abstract: The head keeps the body tracking directly toward the target. If the head veers off to the side, the shoulders and torso will follow. This will misdirect energy, resulting in decreased velocity, accuracy and poor fielding position after the follow through.

Upright Head – Full Explanation

The head and shoulders influence one another, and as such the head can derail the overall energy transfer of the body. The head should remain mostly vertical throughout the delivery – any deviation from vertical arises out of body lean and over-rotation. "Vertical" cannot be maintained 100% of the time, as the head will move slightly laterally as the shoulders tilt and the arm releases the pitch. But, the head should be truly vertical for all of the delivery prior to and following that brief moment when the pitch is released. This reminds us that the shoulders and center of mass are staying on track with the target.

Gloveside body lean   Body aligned directly towards target

The most common manifestation of a tilting head is a pitcher who falls off the mound to his glove side. These pitchers are typically far too rotational, starting with their head and shoulders. Those lacking flexibility and adequate hip and core strength tend to derive power by excessively tilting and rotating their upper body. This not only directs the body's energy on a path away from the plate, but leads to release point and finger placement errors. Typically, pitchers that tilt and pull their head way off their target aren't looking at it. Simply reminding the pitcher to keep his eyes locked on his target will improve compliance greatly, as it's human nature to look at things with a vertical head orientation.

Teaching the Upright Head

The mirror is the best teaching aid to keep the shoulders level and the head vertical. Many pitchers do not realize how severely their head tilts, but seeing it firsthand during mirror drills is the easiest fix. Those with tilting problems simply must continue to focus on pushing the chest forward toward the target, keeping their eyes locked on the target and doing as many mirror drills as possible to reinforce both. It's a good idea to take tape and mark the mirror, showing where the pitcher wants to align his head and shoulders during his delivery. This also requires marking the floor so the pitcher has a set point to start, ensuring he will finish in the same spot each time.

Maxim #9: Late Elbow Quadruple Extension ─────────────

Abstract: The throwing arm should extend directly outward toward the target. During acceleration, a focus on forward extension at release has shown to increase throwing velocity versus a "pulling down" or windmill-like arm path. Pitchers should accelerate their hands directly to the target as hard as possible, holding back extension of the shoulder, elbow, wrist and hand to the last possible moment. This will also produce an ideal follow-through as a side effect.

I have found that pitchers who attempt to pull down on their fastball or who tend to let their elbow extend early during acceleration throw with decreased velocity compared to those focusing on outward extension.

Internal rotation at the shoulder is the fastest human movement. Internal rotation starts to slow when the elbow extends because the lever arm increases, requiring more torque to do the same job. Once the arm is fully straight, internal rotation lasts only briefly longer as the arm adducts and begins to decelerate. Thus, to allow for maximum acceleration, we aim to hold the elbow flexed as long as possible while maintaining height and forward extension, gaining as much velocity as we can from the internal rotators.

Lever arm comparison. Long (bad) on left, good (short) on right.

Achieving Quad-Extension of the Arm

What I believe produces the hardest fastballs is quadruple extension of the four throwing arm joints – the shoulder, elbow, wrist and finger. When all four of these joints release their forward energy in unison, I believe an amplification of power through both muscles and elastic connective tissues occurs. The medieval trebuchet works in a similar manner – using a long lever arm

87

with a shorter, swinging sling that amplifies the power of the long arm. The trebuchet achieves much longer distances by synchronizing two swinging joints as opposed to just one. I believe that throwing with conscious thought regarding the following cues, done repetitiously, will yield the best benefit. Because the movement is high-speed and involves the arm action (which is very difficult to change), low-speed drills have little benefit. Throwing with high focus on the following cues with a radar gun for feedback will yield the best results.

To achieve quad-extension on a fastball, the pitcher must execute four mechanical maxims using the following cues:

1. Keep weight back and shoulders level as long as possible

The weight must explosively shift forward in synchrony with the arm. To do this, the weight must stay back as long as possible while keeping the shoulders level. When the weight shifts forward, the wrist begins to turn over and straighten, which is impossible to rectify – and quad-extension will be lost. The hand can only remain laid back as long as the weight is held back. For cues on this, review maxim #4.

Example of weight staying back (on back leg)

2. Keep the hand behind the ball as long as possible

This cue helps remind the pitcher to be slow early so he can speed up his body late. The sooner the wrist flattens out, the sooner the arm must start decelerating. By keeping the wrist laying back and the fingers behind the ball, the pitcher retains two of the four necessary joint angles to achieve quad-extension.

3. Fingernails forward

The pitcher must drive his chest and hand forward in a low, straight line from high-cocked position to the mitt. I have a special cue for this ("throw with fingernails forward") that helps to keep the pitcher's arm moving directly forward; this will retain elbow flexion longer. The more the hand reaches forward without rotational influence, the longer the elbow will stay flexed, and the better our quad-extension will be.

If the pitcher thinks about keeping his fingernails facing toward the target, his hand cannot pull down, rotate outward, or tense up.

The pitcher will not actually throw with his fingernails forward. But attempting to do so will put his arm on the proper, direct path to the catcher's mitt. And, because the wrist must lay back to deliver the pitch, this layback will be delayed until the very last moment. This will ensure late extension of the wrist, fingers and the elbow joint due to the direct arm path. The last piece of the puzzle, the shoulder, will fully extend naturally if the pitcher throws with 100% effort in a direct line to his target.

4. Extend the elbow like a hinge

With the fingernails forward position, the final goal is to extend the elbow forward like the hinge joint it is. We want to imagine going from the start position below to the finish position as fast as possible. Again – no pulling down, no windmill, no rotation, just direct outward path. While the arm path will not actually look like the photos below, we want to imagine it in this way to best counteract a long, loopy arm path.

Implications of Quad-Extension

If we can synchronize the joint release of all four, we should get an optimally explosive pitch release with base arm speed amplified by the individual acceleration of each joint. As the internal rotation of the shoulder accelerates the hand, the wrist lays back. As the wrist lays back, it must also accelerate forward, exceeding the speed produced by the shoulder. And lastly, as the shoulder starts to extend at the joint, the fingers lay back and then accelerate to give the final push to the ball. The whole process of all four joints extending finally at once will create optimal velocity and spin on the pitch. If any of the four joints gets out of sync with the rest, velocity and ball spin will be reduced.

The Follow Through

Additionally, this momentary explosive acceleration will create a powerful follow through due to late acceleration, one that requires no conscious thought. Those who lack a strong follow through always lack full acceleration to the very release of the pitch. Additionally, poor follow-throughs can be caused by arm tension and recoil, which simply needs to be coached out by verbally reminding the athlete to relax his arm and let it travel as far as it wants to go. The best cue for this is telling the pitcher to allow his arm to follow through until it slaps his own back.

*NOTE – Quad-extension of the arm is a theory, developed through observation and slow-motion photography. I have seen increases in velocity, but no biomechanics research has been conducted to validate it. Try the movement pattern for yourself and see how it works for you.

Pitch Flight Basics
Preface to Chapters 6, 7 & 8

I must define a few terms to most concisely discuss pitch flight. In the following chapters, a chart will be displayed with each pitch to illustrate its unique characteristics. I will then discuss how each of the terms below apply to specific pitches.

Spin Type: The spin of a pitch has a heavy influence on the overall shape of the pitch, the trajectory that it takes as it flies toward the plate.

Backspin: This force provides lift, causing a pitch to resist the force of gravity. A high rate of backspin on a fastball increases perceived velocity.

Topspin: Also known as over spin, this force causes a pitch to break directly downward.

Sidespin: This force causes a pitch move sideways.

Wobblespin: Imparting slight sidespin via offset finger pressure will give the pitch wobbly (relatively slow and tilted) spin that will help it sink and move on a turbulent path through the air. The ball does not actually wobble, but this term helps describe this slower, angular spin rate.

Clock Face Orientation: A clock face is commonly used to describe the shape of a breaking ball.

Clock Illustration showing arrows

Curveball: "12/6" break   "1/7" or "11/5" break

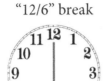 

Changeup,   "2/8" or "10/4" break
Slider,
Sinker:

Fastball: No discernible break

Force Application: This refers to the direction fingertip pressure and hand spin is applied to the baseball. The application of force will determine the spin direction, thus determining the shape and speed of the pitch. Three terms are used in conjunction with an illustration. These terms are universal to righthanders and lefthanders.

Center: Contact finger releases directly in center.
Inner Half: Contact finger releases on the half of the ball closest to the center of the body.
Outer Half: Contact finger releases on half of the ball toward the outside of the body.

Contact Finger: The finger last in contact with the baseball upon release. Note that because the middle finger is the longest, it is almost always the contact finger, and its dominance over the index finger is somewhat dependent on the length disparity between the two.

Speed Differential: The speed reduction from a pitcher's four-seam fastball speed. A four-seam fastball has no differential and is referenced as 100%. All other pitches will be displayed as a percentage of four-seam fastball speed. To determine the speed an offspeed pitch should be thrown, multiply four-seam velocity by the noted percentage.

Depth: This refers to the shape of the pitch. Pitches with more depth have more horizontal or vertical break from a straight line. We want as much depth on offspeed pitches as possible.

Pitch Spin, Flight & Force Application Basics

Optimal pitching first requires an understanding of how the shape of each pitch is created. Energy transmittance is at the forefront of realizing why one pitch takes on its unique shape and speed.

To throw a fastball using 100% of available force, that force must be applied directly through the center of the baseball. This will turn arm and hand speed into two products – linear velocity and backspin, both of which contribute to its straight path through the air.

To make a fastball move, such as in a two-seam fastball, sinker or cut fastball, we have to apply most of the force through the center, with a small amount to the top or side of the ball. Slight force application through the outer side of the ball makes it cut; through the inner side makes it run; through the inner side and top makes it run and sink. These pitches are thus a few percentage points slower than a four-seam fastball.

To throw a curveball, we have to convert a much larger amount of the arm and hand speed into spin. This is done by channeling energy above the baseball via wrist and hand action, which will exchange linear velocity (speed in a straight line) for topspin; this topspin will force the ball to break downward. The more arm speed we can convert into tight topspin, the more sharply the ball will break, and the later during flight it will break – both attributes of an effective curveball. A 12-6 curve needs 100% topspin, while a 1-7 curve needs some of the force applied as sidespin, to make the pitch move laterally while breaking downward. The best curveballs are thrown 15-20% slower than a fastball. This is not because the arm slows down, but because the arm action is different, converting more of the arm's speed to spin.

To throw a slider, which is slower than a fastball but not as slow as a curve, we apply outer-half sidespin and topspin to the ball in almost equal amounts, while applying a more significant amount of force toward the center. This makes the slider a hard pitch – 8-10% slower than a four-seam fastball – and one that has very tight spin. The pitcher must master the delicate balance between applying force diagonally above the ball and yet very close to the center to throw a sharp, late-breaking slider.

Changeups are similar to sliders in that the hand will apply force diagonally to the ball, but the spin is a combination of backspin and wobbly sidespin. This pitch is thrown with 100% arm speed, just like all pitches, but the speed of the pitch is reduced by the hand channeling energy on the side and top of the ball upon release. Good changeups require a very relaxed, fluid hand motion and have a differential of 7-13%, depending on the pitcher and the movement. Much of this speed reduction comes from the movement of the hand and not the grip itself.

CHAPTER 6

THE FASTBALL

To throw an optimal four-seam fastball, 100% of arm speed must be applied directly through the center of the ball; the typical four-seam grip often does not accomplish this. Two-seam fastballs and sinkers are overloaded on the inner half of the ball, adding slight wobblespin and sidespin, which makes the flight of the ball more turbulent and unpredictable. Cut fastballs are loaded slightly on the outer hemisphere, but should only be learned and thrown in the presence of a pitching coach.

The four-seam fastball is the fastest, straightest-flying pitch. It is thrown with backspin and thus has maximum resistance against gravity. There are four variations of the fastball - the four-seam, two-seam, cutter and sinker. Though variations such as the cutter and sinker are more difficult to locate, the fastball in general is the most easily located pitch, regardless of skill level. If a pitcher claims that he can throw an offspeed pitch more reliably for a strike, he has a problem with his mechanics and/or mental approach. Because of the relatively straight flight of the fastball, it should always be the most easily located pitch.

Moreover, the average Major League pitcher throws 65-70% fastballs; amateur players typically throw a percentage of 75-90%. Because it is the most frequently thrown pitch, it follows that fastball mastery has the greatest impact on a pitcher's performance. Thus, mastery of fastball velocity and accuracy should be the #1 concern of all amateur and pro pitchers alike.

The Four-Seam Fastball

Spin:	100% Backspin
Force Application:	Center
Contact Finger:	Middle Finger
Differential:	100%

The four-seam fastball is the fastest and straightest flying fastball; it is thrown with pure backspin. On an ideal fastball, the pitcher the pitcher will apply 100% of his arm speed through the center of the baseball – this is how velocity is maximized. Any energy directed through the sides or over the top of the ball will increase movement but decrease velocity. Sometimes this is an intended consequence, as in the alternate grips shown below, but sometimes it is not.

The Faulty Conventional Four-Seam Grip

The classic four-seam grip does not align the contact finger with the center of the baseball. This grip is typically held with a 1 to 2-finger gap between index and middle, with the gap in the center of the baseball. Because the gap is in the center, the contact finger will release on the descending side on the outer half of the baseball. This will often result in unwanted cutter spin, which both decreases velocity and makes it difficult to locate.

The True Four-Seam Grip

We can improve the backspin and flight of the four-seam fastball by making two slight adjustments:

1. Offset the fingers slightly on the inner half
2. Fingers should be close together – no larger than a one-finger gap

The Two-Seam Fastball

Spin: Backspin/Sidespin Combination
Force Application: Inner half
Contact Finger: Middle Finger
Differential: 97-99%

The two-seam fastball, if thrown properly, should not fly completely straight, but rather move slightly to the arm side. Ideally, this movement will be late and somewhat sharp, but most pitchers will get more of a bearing motion – gradual movement to the pitcher's arm side. It's important to note that proper two-seam movement is run, not cut. A pitch with cutting action moves to the glove side; a pitch that runs moves to the arm side.

There are two different two-seam grips. With both "standard" versions of the grip, we can achieve additional running movement by loading the ball on the inner half. This only requires a slight reorientation of the grip, as shown below.

The "Cross-Seams" Two-Seamer

Grip 1

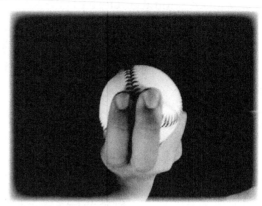

Grip 2

The "With-Seams" Two-Seamer

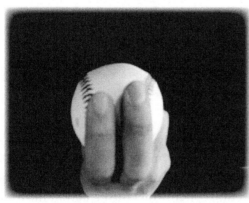

Grip 1

Grip 2

Ones choice of two-seam grip is highly personal. But, one should continually tinker with the grip until the desired results are produced. Some pitchers can make a four-seam fastball run, while others can't make a sinker grip move even an inch. Trial and error is by far the best method to discover and perfect fastball movement – a pitching coach can show the grip, but after that it's all on the pitcher to produce movement.

The Sinking Fastball (Sinker)

Spin: Backspin/Sidespin/Wobblespin Combination
Force Application: Slightly Inner with hand rollover
Contact Finger: Middle Finger
Differential: 96-98%

Grip 1   Grip 2

The "sinker" isn't really a different pitch; in fact, it only becomes a different pitch if it produces the desired result. A pitcher who throws a standard two-seam fastball with tremendous sinking action may refer to it as a sinker; he's not wrong to do so. The sinker is typified by heavy running and sinking action -- not so much by the grip itself. Rule of thumb: if it sinks a lot, it's a sinker. If it doesn't, it's simply a two-seamer.

Yet, the one-seam grip and the heavily offset two-seam grip tend to be the best at producing sink. For this reason, I refer to them as sinker grips. But, if one were to poll ten pitchers who throw sinkers, we might see ten different grips.

The arm-slot and throwing style, as well as setup on the rubber, also has a heavy influence on fastball movement. Pitchers with a lower arm slot will automatically apply more sidespin to the ball (backspin but at an angle), resulting in more lateral movement. Pitchers with lower arm slots are also able to roll their hand over the pitch more easily, imparting a somewhat wobbly sidespin to the ball. Working farther on the gloveside edge of the rubber (discussed in Chapter 1) helps a sinker pitcher roll his hand over the pitch, resulting in greater sinking and running action.

The Cut Fastball (Cutter)

Spin: Backspin/Sidespin Combination
Force Application: Slightly Outer half
Contact Finger: Middle Finger
Differential: 94-97%

           Grip 1   Grip 2

Disclaimer: Few pitchers can properly throw a cut fastball. I believe only collegiate and pro-level pitchers should even attempt this pitch. The cutter is difficult to learn and inappropriate for most pitchers for the following reasons:

1. The cutter is a rare pitch. Few pitchers and pitching coaches have elite-level experience with the cutter, which makes finding proper instruction difficult.

2. The cutter will not move at low speeds. The pitcher has to trust that he is throwing the pitch properly despite getting no visual feedback. Pitchers learn good vs. bad breaking balls by watching them break; this is not possible with the cutter except while throwing at 80%+ intensities. The only feedback mechanism is throwing to a partner who knows what cutter spin should look like (again, a problem – see #1).

3. The cutter must be thrown very hard, with only a 5% differential. Cut must be short and sharp, which, again, is difficult to see. Most pitchers will turn their cutter into a slider so they can see it break and get more swings and misses (see #5).

4. The cutter is a fourth pitch. Most amateur pitchers do not command their fastball & changeup well enough (let alone a third pitch) to worry about adding a fourth to their repertoire. The cutter takes a vast amount of repetition, which should be first applied to developing pro-quality command of a fastball, changeup and traditional breaking ball (curve or slider).

5. The use of aluminum baseball bats makes the cutter slightly less effective as compared to the wood bats used in professional baseball. The cutter is not a swing-and-miss pitch – it is a jam pitch, which lends itself more to wood bats than aluminum bats.

The takeaway: One should not throw a cutter unless he's a pro pitcher or an experienced collegiate pitcher. The pitch is too difficult to learn and is neither necessary nor appropriate for amateur pitchers who aren't, by definition, good enough with the few pitches they do throw. Chances are the reader of this book can't count on more than one hand MLB players who throw a cutter; there's a reason for this.

Screwing Up the Fastball

Unless a pitcher is throwing a cut fastball (which he likely shouldn't as discussed above), the fastball should always be straight or running to the armside. Involuntary cut is one of the biggest fastball flaws.

We don't want fastballs to cut for a few reasons:

1. Movement is unpredictable, so locating the pitch becomes difficult. Usually only some fastballs will cut; if one cuts and the next doesn't, where should the catcher set up to provide the best target? It's a conundrum.
2. Velocity will decrease. A properly thrown cutter will be 3-6% slower than a four-seam fastball. Involuntary cutters will have this same differential, if not more. Pitchers who throw cutting fastballs throw 3-5mph below their potential.
3. It indicates underlying mechanical flaws. An improper grip, flying open, landing open and being over-rotational are what typically lead to involuntary cutters. All of these problems can be solved.

Amateur Pitcher Recommendations

For amateur pitchers throwing below 67mph: Master a four-seam fastball. Don't worry about any other fastball grip.

For amateur pitchers throwing 67+mph: These pitchers should spend their time working on these grips, in order:
1. Four-seam fastball
2. Two-seam fastball
3. Sinker

Why I Recommend These Variations

Amateurs should not throw cutters for reasons discussed above. Those who throw below 67mph will not get much, if any, movement on two-seam or sinker-grip fastballs. These pitchers also need to worry much more about throwing strikes and learning to command a fastball in general. A two-seam fastball is also much more likely to be thrown with involuntary cut as compared to a four-seamer. Thus, I recommend against two-seam fastballs until pitchers can average above 67 miles per hour. The benefit versus cost just isn't high enough on the benefit side.

If a pitcher throws above 67 mph, has good mechanics and consistently throws strikes, he can work on whatever two-seam variation he likes. He will get better movement at speeds in the 70s and 80s, as turbulence on the ball with sidespin and wobblespin increases dramatically. It's important, though, to make sure that his ability to locate his fastball does not decrease as a result of newfound movement.

Coaching the Fastball

We learn a lot about a pitcher by intently watching the ball as he throws, whether during a bullpen or simple game of catch. Pitchers need feedback on the spin of their fastballs – if it's anything less than tight, glassy backspin on a four-seamer, correction to the grip and hand position needs to be made. Any amount of cut should be corrected using the mechanical cues found in chapter five – flying open, over-rotating and/or landing off perpendicular are the most common causes of a pitcher getting unwanted cut on a pitch. Reminding the pitcher to push his chest forward will return his hand to proper position and increase his backspin.

Additionally, pitchers need to be constantly aware of the flight path of their throws. It is very easy, once attention is paid, to determine whether a given throw cuts, runs or flies straight. Amateur pitchers, as discussed in other chapters of this book, too infrequently pay attention to what they're doing; they will throw cutter after cutter, involuntarily, without correction. When asked where their throws are ending up (gloveside) they will then realize what their throws are doing. Correction is often as simple as reinforcing focus on cause and effect. This goes for all pitches, not just the fastball.

FAQ – *Why don't I want cut on the pitch? Mariano Rivera throws a cutter...*

Cut on the ball is a hand and finger position error that will reduce both a pitcher's command of the pitch and its velocity. A cutter, thrown properly by a very hard thrower, will take a short, sharp turn very late in its flight to the plate. This is what makes it very effective – it's thrown hard and breaks very close to the "decision time" of the hitter – the time where he has to choose where to place his bat to hopefully collide with the ball.

Cutters, thrown unintentionally by youngsters, don't have this late break. Rather, they sort of meander slowly across the strike zone. These cutters are slower and, because they are not intentionally thrown, unpredictable.

If one four-seamer flies straight and the next one cuts six inches across the zone, the pitcher will have a hard time judging where his pitches should start and where they will ultimately end up. We want fastballs to be a reliable "strike-getting" pitch – the pitcher knows where to start it and where it will end up. It is my opinion that pitchers should not attempt throwing a true cutter until they have command of an excellent fastball, changeup and traditional breaking ball, and average at least 85mph – qualities of an excellent college or pro pitcher.

CHAPTER 7

THE CHANGEUP

The changeup is thrown with identical arm speed but produces lower release velocity due to two factors: the grip and the action of the hand. The hand must pronate (roll inward) over the ball slightly before release. This, coupled with a relaxed but choking grip, will take 6-12mph off of the pitch and add significant running and sinking movement. The "palm up" mindset is the best cue to throwing an effective changeup.

The Changeup

Spin: Combination Backspin/Wobblespin/Sidespin
Force Application: Inner Half
Contact Finger: Middle and Ring Fingers
Differential: 87-93%

The fundamental offspeed pitch for all ages, the changeup isn't nearly as difficult to learn as many think. The problem is that few know the proper mindset and instructive cues to keep the pitch out of the dirt. Understanding how velocity is taken off the pitch is one of the most crucial aspects in throwing a quality changeup.

Learning and throwing a changeup as a youth is crucial in learning how to pitch in general. Many young pitchers fall in love with the effectiveness of breaking balls at age 11, 12 and 13. Because hitters can't hit "crooked" pitches at a young age, youth pitchers favor them over the straighter changeup. Changeups have significantly less break than a curveball or slider. Because of this, a pitcher throwing a changeup learns more about the way speed change alone affects a hitter. If a young pitcher can learn to get outs with a changeup and fastball, he will be even more capable when he adds a breaking pitch to his arsenal later on. And, as hitters learn to hit breaking balls with age and experience, pitchers with only mediocre curves and sliders suddenly find themselves with very few tools to get outs against increasingly skilled hitters.

The "Hook 'em Horns" Changeup Grip

I use what I refer to as a "Hook 'em horns" grip. The steps in initially finding the grip are as follows:

1. Make the "Hook 'em horns" symbol

2. Turn the palm up, keep middle and ring finger together

3. Lay the fingers down on the ball with middle fingers and thumb opposed

4. Index finger and pinky lay gently on the ball

5. Use a with-seams grip.

Changeup Grip Notes:

- The middle fingers should sit between the seams of the ball. But, if this isn't comfortable, variations of the grip will work – four-seam or cross-seams grip will do.
- The ball must be held as loosely as possible while being choked.
- The ball must sit deeply in the hand - it should be in contact with the lowest finger digits.
- Do not force the index finger and pinky down the sides of the ball – this will create tension in the hand.

Throwing the Changeup: Hand Action Cues

As mentioned earlier, the changeup will be thrown with reduced speed due to two factors – the grip and the hand action. Each of these contributes about 50% to speed reduction, but the hand action is the main contributor of spin and movement to the pitch. While speed change is crucial, the movement of the pitch is what transforms an ordinary changeup into a legendary one.

Cue #1: Palm Up

"Palm up" is the most effective cue for the changeup because it softens and puts the hand in position to create optimum pronation over the ball. This cue will also prevent the ball from being involuntarily thrown in the dirt, solving arguably the biggest problem beginners face throwing a changeup – bouncing it. This is because when the wrist is stiff, the fingers tend to stiffen as well, creating a rigid, claw-like hand that will likely force the ball down into the ground.

Bad (stiff) wrist

Good (relaxed) wrist

Cue #2: Thumb Down

"Thumb down" also contributes to relaxing the hand, which forces the fingers to relax and helps prevent bouncing the pitch. Forcefully pulling the thumb down immediately opens the hand (try it), which is why this cue is so effective at relaxing the hand and wrist.

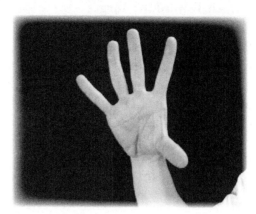

Thumb being "pulled" down to open the hand.

Cue #3: Palm Away

Pronation over the ball is one of the most crucial factors in reducing velocity and adding movement to the changeup. We want the pitcher to pronate slightly earlier than he naturally would, which will impart more sidespin and wobblespin. If the pitcher is finishing with his palm facing the target while learning the pitch, he's not applying as much pronation as is required. Finishing with a palm facing the third baseman (righthanders) or the first baseman (lefthanders) makes a tremendous difference.

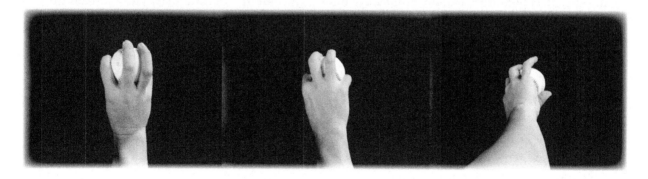

Throwing the Changeup: Body Action Cues

I use two main cues for the body, both of which influence the release point and the action of the hand.

Cue #1: Reach Toward the Target

While this is a cue we want to use on every single pitch, I see changeups go awry when pitchers get too much of the "windmill" type arm action. We don't want to pull down on our pitches – we want to force them through the zone by extending toward the target. The pitcher needs to think out toward the target; hand straight to the mitt.

When the pitcher pulls down on his changeup, the wrist stiffens and fingers force the ball into the dirt, much like an eagle's talons. If the arm is pulling the ball down like a windmill, all of the hand action cues become ineffective, and the pitch turns flat, hard and difficult to throw for a strike.

Cue #2: Chest and Core Crunch Forward

This cue helps get extension through the target and helps keep the hand on top of the ball. We don't want any extra rotation in the delivery, as discussed in the mechanics chapter. Excess rotation has a very negative effect on the changeup. It causes the hand to supinate (turn thumb toward outside of body) before release, ruining the pitcher's ability to pronate over the pitch. The #1 cause of inconsistent changeup movement is inconsistent mechanics – those who don't consistently push their chests forward end up with different hand position on nearly every pitch, resulting in poor control and unpredictable movement.

When the chest goes forward, the hand stays on top the ball in a neutral orientation. From this position, we can then drive the hand toward the target and use our hand cues properly. This will result in a changeup with consistent velocity and consistent movement.

Throwing the Changeup: Mental Cues

Cue #1: Think Fastball

The idea that the changeup is a "fastball with a different grip" is wrong considering the way we physically throw the pitch – the hand action is drastically different and throwing it like a fastball will yield a flat, ineffective changeup. However, having the fastball mindset is absolutely critical in throwing the changeup properly.

"Think fastball" refers to not getting caught up in trying to make the changeup move or slow down. Too often, pitchers have mastered the grip and hand action but get anxious before throwing the pitch. Nervous energy with offspeed pitches – typically because the pitcher isn't confident he can throw it where he wants it or with enough speed reduction – will create tension in the arm, causing the pitch to hang. The more relaxed the pitcher is, the more loose his arm and hand will be, allowing the changeup to be released properly.

Pitchers often suffer from "offspeed pitch anxiety," caused by a pitcher overthinking the location and difficulty of throwing an offspeed pitch. If there is no physical or mechanical flaw behind a pitch, the problem is simply angst and the subsequent tension created, that causes a pitch to be thrown improperly. The typical result is a changeup that hangs up in the zone and to the armside of the plate. Tension from anxiety flows through the arm and prevents the pitcher from staying relaxed while reaching full extension; this causes the pitch to hang. This is much more frequent a problem than people realize – when mechanics look okay but the pitch is thrown poorly, the problem is likely mental.

Cue #2: Adjust the Focal Point

Focal point is critical on breaking balls and fastballs and changeups with movement; they have a different starting and ending point. If the changeup sinks and runs five inches diagonally to the armside, the pitcher must start the pitch five inches diagonally to the gloveside; we need to account for movement if the pitch is to end up in the proper location. This is discussed in higher detail in chapter nine.

An all-too-common error is the pitcher not adjusting for the movement of his pitch; this is critical. The easiest fix for a changeup bouncing in the dirt is for the pitcher to simply raise his eyes to a higher focal point (throat of the catcher is usually the right height). If he aims for the mitt and bounces the pitch, aiming for the throat should "vector" the pitch so that it sinks right into the mitt. Raising the focal point also helps a pitcher who is pulling down too much to gain more extension toward the plate.

Cue #3: Throw Harder and Accelerate Late

Because the changeup is mostly straight, pitchers fear throwing the pitch too hard. Often, this results in "babying" the pitch – throwing it with less than 100% arm speed. Throwing the pitch at a reduced relative intensity results in a flat pitch with little deception – the exact opposite of what is desired. The pitch's effectiveness diminishes exponentially as the arm slows down because less pronation and spin is applied to the ball.

The mindset for the changeup should be to throw it 105% as hard as the fastball, with explosive late acceleration of the arm and hand. This will make the hand action as dynamic as possible, which will impart the most spin and create the most deceptive pitch possible. Fast arm + slow pitch – that's the perfect recipe for a changeup.

Screwing Up the Changeup

All problems with the changeup can be solved with the above cues. Most pitchers who struggle to throw consistently effective changeups exhibit one of the following problems, in descending order of prevalence:
1. Lack of sufficient repetition and focus
2. Stiff wrist on release and windmill action
3. Insufficient energy over the ball
4. Anxiety about the risk of the pitch

Solving the Problems Above

#1: Lack of sufficient repetition and focus

This is simple – throw more changeups and ensure that every single one is thrown with proper hand action. The changeup needs to be thrown during catch, during bullpens and during games. Many young pitchers will claim that they don't need to throw changeups in their games because their fastball is so effective. Amateurs who throw exceptionally hard are often correct in this claim, but they will eventually reach a level where their fastball will not dominate. Yet, they need to work in the changeup if they expect to improve on the pitch. If the goal is to be a next-level pitcher, all offspeed pitches must be thrown during a game, even if one could dominate with only a fastball. It won't improve if it's never thrown.

#2: Stiff wrist on release; windmill action

The stiff wrist will cause the pitch to be thrown too hard, too flat, and down in the dirt more often than not. To combat this, the pitcher must work on keeping his palm up as long as possible, pulling the thumb down to open the hand and allow the ball to roll off softened fingers. This will set the stage to finish with palm away. Pushing the chest toward a higher focal point will keep the pitch sinking to the mitt and out of the dirt.

Example of a stiff (poor) wrist

#3: Insufficient energy over the ball

Some pitchers have difficulty with the changeup because of a.)poor wrist flexibility and b.) fastball-like (through the ball) finish. Finishing over the changeup requires hand action that's smooth and relaxed, much like using a paintbrush. Those who are too stiff-wristed, tense and rigid in their finish struggle with both speed differential and movement. Focusing on a soft, relaxed, palm-away finish while playing catch with the changeup will yield good results for these pitchers.

#4: Mental anxiety about the risk of the pitch

A relaxed hand and arm starts with a relaxed mind. Many pitchers are uncertain about their ability, or perceived inability, to locate offspeed pitches. This tension becomes a self-fulfilling prophecy, as it locks the body up and prevents proper action and finish on a pitch.

When a pitcher can throw a changeup well in catch but not in a bullpen, or well in a bullpen but not in a game, the only variable is the mentality. It's normal to get nervous in competition; the pitcher just needs reminding that the changeup mindset is the same as the fastball – relax, trust it and throw with confidence.

FAQ – *I have a different changeup grip that I prefer. Do the cues included in this book still apply?*

Absolutely. There are many ways to throw a changeup. The grip I teach is what I consider to be the best of all worlds – easy to learn with great movement and deception. However, I know that it won't work for everyone.

If you have a different changeup grip, the cues included in this book will still work – use them for troubleshooting regardless of how you hold the pitch. While the right grip is a big piece of the puzzle, the hand and body actions involved are by far the most important factors. If you're struggling with my grip, the reason is likely your hand and body action, not the grip itself.

FAQ – *Can I tweak the "Hook 'em Horns" changeup grip?*

Again, the answer is yes, and I highly recommend tinkering with the grip to find the best one for you. Many pitchers have one grip that they'll use when they want a called strike (less movement) and another grip they'll use to try to bury the pitch for a strikeout. Having variations of the same grip that produce varying levels of movement is very advantageous. Never stop experimenting!

CHAPTER 8

THE CURVEBALL

The curveball can be difficult to learn if the physics, arm and hand action aren't clearly understood. The curve must be thrown with a "waterfall" mentality, creating a sweeping, circular arm path that converts high amounts of arm and hand speed into topspin. While the pitch should be thrown as hard as possible, the arm action differs significantly from the fastball.

The Curveball

Spin:	Topspin or topspin with slight sidespin
Force Application:	Center
Contact Finger:	Second knuckle of middle finger
Differential:	80-85%

The Lost Art

The curveball is becoming a lost art due to the prevalence of the slider. The slider can be thrown with a similar arm path as the fastball, which makes it more easily learned by less athletic pitchers. Those who throw curveballs must possess the ability to differentiate arm action between the fastball and curveball automatically while in a game – a difficult task. While only the curveball will be taught in this book, the slider can be a suitable breaking ball if throwing properly.

The correct age to learn (read – learn – not rely upon) the curveball is 15-16 years old, depending on physical maturity. While growth plates may still be open at this age, it's impractical to continue to hold a freshman or sophomore back from throwing a breaking ball. Scouts will start to make their rounds at these ages, so it's good to show some feel for a breaking ball, even if it's just here and there. Skeletal immaturity, inexperience, and improper technique increase the risk placed on the arm. Inexperienced pitchers will often throw way too many curveballs per game; skeletal immaturity places more stress on growth plates and other weak tissues; improper technique places much more torque on the elbow and shoulder joints (e.g. the "little league curve").

Again, when I say that 15 to 16 is the correct age to learn the curve, I do mean learn. This cannot be emphasized enough, as many amateurs fall in love with breaking balls as soon as they discover the grip. The focus should still be chiefly on the changeup until 17-18 years old, at which time growth plates are more likely to be close and the curveball can start to share the spotlight.

Shape and Speed

A good curveball has the biggest shape of any breaking ball but should not be loopy. The curve must be thrown as hard as possible to prevent it from "popping" up out of the hand. Slowly thrown curve balls will pop upward out of the hand, making them easy to recognize. The harder the curveball is thrown, the later and more sharply it will break. Good curveballs appear to break straight down in a sharp angle toward the ground. The term "drop off the table" is apt – quality curveballs are very difficult to hit and break very sharply downward.

Slow curveballs are never as sharp as harder-thrown ones; the pitcher must focus at all times on throwing the pitch as hard as he throws his fastball. But, because the arm action is different, it can be difficult to find the middle ground between throwing the pitch hard and still getting it to break properly – this is why many pitchers give up learning the curveball.

Don't Throw the "Little League Curve"

The "little league curve" refers to the side-torqued curveball thrown by amateur pitchers. As discussed below, the pro-style curveball has a hand action that channels energy over the ball, imparting topspin. The little league curve is torqued sideways, like turning a doorknob, and imparts sidespin. Many young pitchers lack the proprioception and body control to properly throw the pro-style curve; as such, curveballs should be avoided altogether.

The Pro Curveball Grip

I use a four-seam curveball grip, which is achieved by creating a tightly wedged C with the hand. The steps for finding the grip are as follows:

Step 1: Find four-seam orientation.

Step 2: Wedge the ball in tightly between the middle and ring finger.

Step 3: Relax the hand over the ball, parallel with the four-seam orientation.

Step 4: Apply pressure via the middle finger.

Step 5: Index finger must not apply pressure. There are four placement options to prevent applying pressure – fingers cross, stick up, "knuckle" or sit lightly on the ball.

Step 6: Hand rotates forward over the ball

Curveball Grip Notes

- The ball must be jammed deep into the crook of the index and ring finger. However, the hand as a whole should be relaxed and loose.
- The four-seam grip is ideal because it will make the spin look tighter as the ball rotates, mirroring a four-seam fastball and making the curveball harder for the batter to pick up.
- Index finger placement is important – index finger pressure will soften the break of the pitch. To obtain the sharpest break possible, the middle finger should act as a knife-edge with little to no pressure coming from the index finger.
- The four methods of lifting the index finger from the ball are entirely individual – the pitcher should tinker and choose the most comfortable method.

Throwing the Curveball: Hand Action Cues

The curveball has far more arm action and mental cues than hand action cues, as the hand plays a lesser role in the pitch. The pitcher needs good wrist flexibility, however, if he is going to impart maximum spin on the ball. Simple wrist stretching will help.

Cue #1: Fingers on Top

I've watched hundreds of thousands of throws leave the hands of pitchers. The common denominator of a sharp-breaking curve versus a soft-breaking one is finger placement. Because the arm will be channeling energy over the top the ball, the fingers must be on the same plane. If the wrist rotates around the side of the ball rather than over the top, the sidespin will not match the topspin produced by the arm. If the spin from both the arm action and hand action match, spin rate will increase significantly and the pitch will have much sharper break.

Poor release. Fingers on the side of the ball.

Good release. Fingers on top.

Cue #2: Second Knuckle Forward

This cue is an extension of the fingers on top cue. If the pitcher takes his second knuckle toward his target, he will keep his fingers on top of the ball and will keep his hand tracking perfectly toward the target.

Throwing the Curveball: Arm Action & Body Cues

Arm action on the curveball varies greatly from that of the fastball. Improvements in arm action will yield the biggest gains in curveball tightness, shape and consistency.

Cue #1: Elbow at Upside-Down 7

Proper elbow shape as the arm starts to rotate forward is about 70-90° flexion of the elbow. The extension of the elbow at release increases the spin on the pitch, and must coincide with the release of the hand over the ball.

Cue #2: Bicep Squeeze

Pitchers who extend their elbows early are forced to rely solely on their hand and wrist for spin, which is not enough to create good topspin. For those pitchers who extend too early, asking them to squeeze their biceps helps build the feel for keeping the elbow flexed as long as possible.

Cue #3: Arm Relaxes as it Travels Forward

The arm must stay relaxed until it starts to reach toward the target. If the arm accelerates early, it will push the pitch into the upper parts of the zone. Early acceleration is one of the biggest reasons curveballs "hang" in the upper parts of the strike zone.

Cue #4: Reach over the Pitch

This is where the curve really starts to differ from the fastball – at release. The pitcher must feel his hand reach above the ball rather than through the center of it.

Cue #5: Stay Down the Shoulder

Pitchers tend to accelerate too early with both the arm and the chest – if the upper body rotates open (flies open) too soon, the pitch will almost always hang up toward the armside of the plate. This is because as the chest rotates open, the arm lags behind and accelerates to catch up. Because it can't catch up with the chest, the arm and pitch will push upward.

Cue #6: Chest Forward

This is a cue that recurs for every single pitch, but that's because the implications are huge. Pushing the chest forward will prevent over-rotation that forces a pitcher to get on the side of the ball, lessening its bite and causing a soft-breaking sweeping motion.

Throwing the Curveball: Mental Cues

Mental cues are extremely important for the curveball because they can make the difference in getting the arm and hand action cues right. A proper mindset of throwing the pitch will increase compliance with the teaching points.

Mental Cue #1: Stay Relaxed; Let the Arm Travel

This is both an arm-action cue and a mental cue because the error in early acceleration is often a result of an anxious pitcher. Pitchers who get excited about the idea of breaking off a nasty curveball will almost always jump the gun, so to speak, and try to execute the pitch too early in the delivery. A pitcher has to act like a cheetah hiding in tall grass – wait, wait, wait, pounce! The arm has to be relaxed all the way up until it begins to reach toward the plate, at which time the arm accelerates powerfully above the ball, pulling down hard.

If a pitcher's curveball is chronically hanging up and to the armside, it's highly likely that the pitcher is accelerating too early, and he needs to relax his arm and wait to accelerate until later in the delivery.

Mental Cue #2: Visualize a Round Pitch Shape

While we want the curveball to thrown hard with a very jagged, sharp break, visualizing roundness will help remind the pitcher to channel his arm speed above the ball. Most curveballs that bounce are a result of a pitcher putting his arm speed through the ball, rather than over top of it.

Mental Cue #3: The Waterfall Method

The waterfall is a great curveball analogy; the cliff is an abruptly explosive endpoint to a slowly meandering river. The water casually rolls down the river before accelerating downward all at once.

Think of the arm path as a waterfall: relaxed and slow until the arm reaches forward extension, and then BOOM – sudden, explosive arm acceleration pulls down on the ball, imparting tremendous spin. If there is one mental cue to use, this is the one.

Mental Cue #4: Higher Focal Point

Many pitchers struggle to keep their curve out of the dirt because they stare exclusively at the mitt. If the pitcher uses the mitt as his starting point with a curve that breaks 16 inches, the ball will end up 16 inches below the mitt, which will be in the dirt.

A simple solution that allows the pitcher to feel comfortable pulling hard on the pitch is to raise the focal point. Pulling hard downward on a curve that starts at the catcher's mask will still end up in the strike zone, no matter how hard the pitcher tries to pull.

The focal point, as discussed in chapter nine, is crucial for locating breaking pitches.

Putting it All Together: Summary of the Pro-Style Curve

Step 1: Get the proper grip.
Step 2: Elbow stays tight in an upside-down "7" as arm moves forward.
Step 3: Arm stays relaxed and does not accelerate during early movement toward the plate.
Step 4: Elbow angle must extend at exact moment the hand rolls forward over the top of the ball.
Step 5: "Waterfall" time – once arm starts to reach forward, pull down hard on the ball.
Step 6: Accelerate the arm out and down as much as possible into the follow through

Screwing up the Curveball

Pitchers who throw ineffective curveballs will fall into one of the following categories:
1. Soft-breaking; can throw it for strikes
2. Soft-breaking; cannot throw it for strikes
3. Medium or hard-breaking; cannot throw it for strikes

What a pitcher wants is a hard-breaking curve that he can throw for strikes. Most fall short of this. The most common problems with those that throw ineffective curveballs are the following:

1. Hangs the pitch too often
2. Throws pitch in the dirt too often
3. Pitch has depth but has soft break
4. Pitch is flat and has little depth
5. Pitch is easily recognized

Solving the Above Problems

#1: Hangs the pitch too often

A "hanging" curve refers to one that is left up in the strike zone with soft-breaking action. There are two root causes for those who hang the curveball too often; the first is early acceleration of the arm. The second is flying open too early and over-rotating.

A pitcher who hangs curveballs needs to be reminded to stay down his front shoulder as long as possible and to push his chest forward instead of spinning toward the plate. Over-rotation will pull the front shoulder and chest out, causing the arm to lag behind and the curveball to hang.

Early acceleration is probably the greater problem, and it requires a mixture of mental and arm-action cues. The pitcher must remind himself to stay relaxed with his arm and allow it to travel forward, slowly, and reach to the target before he accelerates. The arm can only accelerate and get on top of the pitch if it's already leading out toward the plate. The waterfall visualization works wonders – the pitcher should visualize his arm traveling slowly forward before violently pulling down when the "cliff" is reached.

#2: Throws pitch in the dirt too often

Pitchers who can't get the curveball to the catcher in the air usually struggle because they don't channel arm speed above of the baseball; they throw too much through the pitch. The arm action on the curve is different than the fastball – it requires a pitcher to reach up and over the ball before pulling down.

The pitcher should be thinking about creating more depth on the pitch by visualizing a round shape. If his mind is thinking round, his arm will be more apt to follow a round path. The waterfall visualization is also helpful in breaking the straight-to-the-target habit.

Focal point must also raise up. This is an easy fix because, if this pitcher starts the pitch higher, it will have more room for error in its downward break. Starting the pitch at the mitt means it will almost always break into the dirt. This is good when a pitcher wants a strikeout, but not when a pitcher needs contact or a called strike.

Lastly, pitchers who are too tense and over-grip the ball will force it straight into the ground, even if all other mechanical and mental cues are good. The ball needs to be minimally gripped – only as tightly as is needed to keep it in the hand.

#3: Pitch has depth (relatively large break) but soft break

If the curve has depth but isn't sharp (a loopy curveball), then the pitcher needs to speed his arm up and throw the pitch harder. The grip and arm action should also be analyzed to make sure the elbow isn't straightening out too soon. If the hand and arm action are incorrect, as discussed above, then the upside-down 7 and bicep tightness cues should be used. The hand and wrist must be loose and flexible to impart maximum spin on the ball, even as the arm speeds up. Many pitchers, when attempting to throw a curveball harder, will tense up; this will decrease spin and result in a harder but flat curveball. It takes repetition to find the balance between throwing the curve as hard as possible while also staying loose and relaxed.

#4: Pitch is flat and has little depth

As mentioned in #3, pitchers who throw their curveball with too much tension in their body and hand will bounce the pitch often. The curve should not be gripped too tightly.
Pitchers who throw their curveball for strikes with a flat shape do a lot of things correctly – they stay closed, don't fly open and usually reach to the plate fairly well. But, what they lack is quality shape of the pitch – a higher focal point and focus on pitch roundness and a waterfall mindset will go a long way.

The biggest reason behind curve flatness is a lack of energy over the ball. The pitch cannot be forced forward like a fastball or else too little energy will be converted into topspin. Again, a focus on shaping the pitch is paramount, as well as keeping the bicep angle tight, at the upside-down 7 position as long as possible.

#5: Pitch is easily recognized and is hit hard

This flaw implies two things: the curve is popping up out of the hand, and it isn't breaking sharply. Throwing the pitch as hard as possible, while maintaining a waterfall mindset, will force the pitch forward out of the hand, preventing the ball from popping up. Higher velocity pitches also appear straight longer, making a later, more sudden break. Throwing a curveball as hard as possible is absolutely crucial. A pitcher should continue to increase his curve speed until he can throw it at an 85% differential.

FAQ – *What's the difference between a curve and a knuckle curve?*

There is none. Spiking the fingertip into the ball prevents the index finger from putting pressure in the center of the ball, which as discussed above, will help create a middle finger knife-edge. The knife-edge is crucial to creating tight spin on the curveball, but the knuckle placement itself does nothing more to increase the break of the pitch. Some say that the index finger flicks the ball to increase spin, but this is ludicrous – even an average curveball is thrown with one to two thousand r.p.m, and a flick of the fingernail would do nothing to amplify such an already high spin rate. Plus, the finger would have to flick sideways against the natural hinging direction of the finger joint to match the topspin direction. Knuckle contribution is a myth.

FAQ – *Should I throw a slower "get-me-over" curveball when I need a strike?*

No. Again, as mentioned earlier, slowly thrown curveballs pop up out of the hand, making them easy to recognize and hit. Additionally, hitters will quickly realize that a pitcher slows down on his curveball when he needs a strike, so they will look for the ball to pop up and then swing for the fences. Pitchers should always throw their best version of the curveball and should learn to differentiate locations by using their focal point to start the pitch in a location that will allow it to break to the desired end point.

FAQ – *What type of break is best? Is 12-6 better than 1-7?*

There is no single, correct break for all pitchers, and the answer will be revealed by watching the action of the pitch. A pitcher should tinker with different planes of break and talk with his catcher, pitching coach and teammates to discuss which pitch is sharper and more deceptive. Because each pitcher's arm action and arm slot is unique, there is no way to predict which plane will produce the sharpest break – some pitchers throw sharper curves at 12-6 while some have sharper break at a 1-7 plane.

But, there is one absolute: Two-plane break is more difficult to hit than single-plane break. A 12-6 curve breaks in one plane: straight down. A 1-7 curve breaks down and to the gloveside, so the hitter's brain has extra physics work to discern where the pitch will end up. While two-plane break is ideal, sharpness and lateness of break should be the pitcher's first priority.

CHAPTER 9

TARGET ALIGNMENT SYSTEM

HOW WE (ACTUALLY) THROW STRIKES

Alignment of three crucial body parts allows the pitcher to throw the ball to the desired location; these bodyparts are the eyes, shoulders and chest. Although many errors may derail the pitcher and cause missed pitch locations, consistent alignment means consistent accuracy. Adjusting the focal point to better guide pitches to the desired target location is how good pitchers adjust to errors in the targeting system.

One overlooked aspect of pitching mechanics is the actual mechanism of throwing strikes. While having repeatable, consistent mechanics is important, it's only half of the equation. We have to ask ourselves how the pitcher is able to differentiate his pitches – high, low, in and out. How does a pitcher actually make a pitch go to one spot or another?

Pre-Pitch Visualization

This is the blueprint behind a pitch – pitchers who are more in tune with their minds will visualize the exact shape and location of every pitch. It's almost like a catalog of pitches – the pitcher nods his head for curveball down and away, and immediately the visual image of a curveball breaking sharply down and away pops into the mind. The more vivid the pre-pitch image, the more likely the pitcher is to execute the pitch the way he envisions it.

Visual Targeting Via the Focal Point

When the pitch is chosen, the visual targeting system takes over. It's crucial for the pitcher not only to visualize where his pitch will end up, but also to lock eyes on the location where the pitch will start. Focal point is the term for the spot on which the pitcher will lock his eyes as the starting point for the pitch. Target refers to the end location of the pitch (usually, but not always, the catcher's mitt).

Triangle = focal point. Circle = target.
Example of adjusting for a breaking pitch.

Triangle = focal point. Circle = target.
Example of overlap for a fastball (no break).

The focal point must be adjusted for the amount of break likely to result; if the pitch breaks downward 10 inches, then the focal point should be 10 inches above the desired location. The only way for a pitcher to adjust his location is by trial and error – he picks a focal point, throws his pitch, and assesses where the pitch ends up. If the pitch ended up in an unintended location, he will then analyze his mechanics and the shape of the pitch to determine what needs to improve in the delivery of the next pitch.

Some pitchers pick up their target early before their delivery, and some look away briefly as the leg kicks before reconnecting with the focal point. Regardless of the method used, the pitcher should have a strong visual connection with his focal point to engage with it as long and as firmly as possible.

Three-Part Alignment

Once the focal point is chosen, the pitcher must somehow get his body to throw to that exact, often tiny, location. To do this, the pitcher must align three parts of his body with the focal point during his delivery to the plate.

Part 1: The Eyes

The eyes must lock on the focal point and stay strongly engaged with it for the duration of the pitch. If the eyes cannot lock on the focal point, the body will be like a ship without a captain – without direction.

Part 2: The Shoulders

The torso will always follow the shoulders; when the shoulders stay closed to the target, so must the torso. When the shoulders align with the focal point, so must the torso.

Because the shoulders will steer the rest of the body into position, they must point directly at the focal point. This means for balls up in the zone, the shoulders maintain a slightly higher angle. For balls headed down in the zone, the shoulders should tilt slightly lower.

Understand, however, that shoulder alignment should happen automatically if the pitcher is visually engaged with the focal point.

Part 3: The Chest

The chest, signifying the center of mass, is far and away the most important element of the alignment system. Even if the eyes and shoulders lock and track to the focal point, the chest can, and often does, derail the pitch from its course.

The chest must push directly forward to the focal point. The eyes lock, the shoulders track the torso, and finally the center of the chest drives to the focal point.

When the pitcher flies open and over-rotates, the chest will veer away from the focal point, taking the arm and baseball with it. Because the arm is connected with the torso, it will always follow the center of mass. If the center of mass drives toward the focal point, so will the arm.

Putting it All Together

If the three parts of the system align – eyes, shoulders and chest – the pitcher will throw accurately with consistency. But, there are many reasons the pitcher's targeting system will misalign, causing erratic control and missed locations.

What About the Stride?

The stride will be mostly constant with only minute, imperceptible differences in pitch location. While the stride will follow the direction of the eyes and shoulders, it will still land in nearly the exact same spot on every pitch, give or take an inch or two. The directional differentiation of one pitch to the next is physically made in the shoulders and the chest – the chest will push slightly toward the location, even though the stride lands in a somewhat neutral location.

Screwing up the Target Alignment System

A number of common errors may cause a pitcher's targeting system to misalign, resulting in errors in location.

#1: Rotation error

The chest must drive forward to the focal point. As mentioned above, if the torso is too rotational, the center of mass will veer away from the focal point, taking the arm with it and causing a missed location.

Example of a rotation error resulting in arm drag

#2: Arm swing error

The arm is not mentioned in the alignment system because it should come into position naturally. However, pitchers often get lazy with the backswing of their arm, preventing it from attaining the high cocked position when the body is ready to accelerate. Sometimes, the pitcher is sluggish in bringing his arm up, and simply breaking the hands and moving the hands up faster will remedy the problem.

However, mound height is a typical culprit when pitchers fall off-rhythm with their arm swing. Atypically high mounds keep the pitcher in the air longer during the stride, which disrupts the timing of the hand break and arm swing. Unusually low mounds force the pitcher to land sooner, which means the normal cadence of the arm swing will not be fast enough to reach normal height. These mound errors, however, are usually remedied within a few pitches or batters – a pitcher must adapt quickly to sort out his timing.

Another common source of arm swing errors is switching from the windup to the stretch. Stride air-time is very different when changing from high leg kick to slide step, often affecting arm swing timing.

#3: Fatigue error

Fatigue may prevent a pitcher from reaching optimal height on his arm swing, which will cause an arm swing error. Pitchers also tend to rotate more as they tire, an attempt to gather more power from the core when fatigued. This will cause a rotation error. Lastly, leg fatigue will negatively affect stride length and forward momentum, which in turns prevents the torso and chest from pushing forward to the target, resulting in balls left up in the zone.

#4: Visual error

If the eyes don't pick up the target soon enough, it is almost guaranteed that the pitch will end up in a random location. The pitcher still may throw the ball in or around the strike zone, but full control over the pitch is impossible. Pitchers will sometimes lose focus and fail to pick up the focal point adequately, which will result in a visual error and loss of accuracy.

#5: Head error

Head errors are a combination of a visual error and a rotation error in which the head pulls to the gloveside, causing the center of mass to go with it. Pitchers who excessively tilt the shoulders and head to the gloveside usually have difficulty throwing strikes.

Example of excessive head tilt resulting in poor release

#6: Stride error

The stride foot should consistently land toward the center of the plate, which is a neutral location. However, some amateur pitchers will close off too much (landing too far on the armside of the body), stride too far to the gloveside (landing too open), or present other variations in their stride length or direction. A stride error is one in which the body can't track effectively to the target because the stride foot lands too far from neutral. Common example: pitchers who land too closed cannot locate well, if at all, to the gloveside third of the plate. This is because they increase the distance their body must rotate to reach a release point on the gloveside of the plate.

#7: Leg drive error

This is typically, but not always, a sign of fatigue – when the legs don't propel the pitcher down the mound as forcefully as normal, the arm lags and the chest will not drive adequately forward. The pitcher will often tilt his shoulders upward to combat this leg fatigue, resulting in a severe breakdown of the targeting system. This error is produced by fatigue, laziness or lack of proper teaching on how to use the legs.

The Vector System – Intentional Erroneous Focal Points

The reality is that big league pitchers aren't capable of throwing a strike 100% – or even 75% – of the time, on average. And, major leaguers hit their spot exactly much, much less than that. But, knowing how to adjust from missed locations is a huge part of being a good pitcher. Changing the focal point to account for the break of the pitch is a sensible and necessary move. But on fastballs, where the focal point is the target, the pitcher must choose a focal point that matches his typical miss, a phenomenon I call vectoring. Good pitchers adjust their focal point to accommodate an expected miss of location when they can't find a mechanical fix to solve the accuracy problem.

Let's use an example to explain:

A pitcher aims to throw a fastball to his catcher's mitt down the middle of the plate. Upon delivering the pitch, he misses badly high – about 18 inches above his target. Assuming he can't get his mechanics to adjust, the pitcher must pick a location that will account for his miss, even if it's severe. Assuming the catcher's mitt isn't 18 inches off the ground when set up for a low strike, the pitcher must pick a spot on the ground to account for his typical 18-inch miss. This pitcher intently stares at the front edge of the plate as he attempts his next fastball. Because he misses well high of his target, his "miss" is now a strike – the focal point placed on the plate allowed him to miss it high, which then becomes a low strike.

The vectoring system works remarkably well not just for breaking pitches, but also for days when the pitcher struggles to locate in general. By defining a pattern of misses, the pitcher can accurately choose new focal points that allow him to "miss" into the strike zone.

CHAPTER 10
PITCH SEQUENCE & LOCATION

Logical pitch sequences save runs. The goal of any pitch sequence is to disrupt a hitter's timing, making him uncomfortable and indecisive. Moving the ball in and out, up and down, while changing speeds and mixing pitches, will accomplish these goals.

Pitch Location Basics

Every pitcher must master a handful of locations for each pitch in his arsenal. For each location, the pitch will take a slightly different shape, making it essentially a different pitch altogether.

The Fastball

Variation #1: "Called Strike" Fastball

Counts used: 2-0, 3-0, 3-1
- This fastball will be thrown down the middle when the pitcher is way behind on the count and desperately needs a strike.
- Typical location: Down the middle
- Sorry, but because you fell way behind, you don't have a choice.

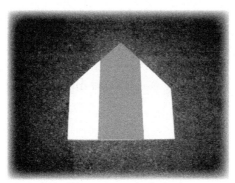

Pitch location = dark shade

Variation #2: "Contact" Fastball

Counts used: 0-0, 1-0; 1-1; 2-1; 3-2
- This fastball is not a "gimme," but also needn't be too precise. When even or slightly behind in the count, the pitcher should move the ball slightly off the middle of the plate while still giving himself a lot of plate to work with.
- Typical Location: Inner or outer halves

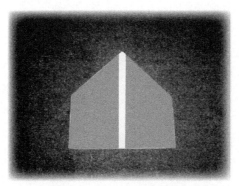

Pitch location = dark shade

Variation #3: "Ahead in the Count" Fastball

Counts used: 0-1; 1-2; 2-2
  • The pitcher has worked himself ahead in the count, so the hitter should not see a pitch anywhere near the heart of the plate. As the pitcher gets farther ahead, his pitches should move progressively toward the edges of the plate
  • Typical Location: Inner or outer thirds
  • Note: 2-2, while an even count, is included here because the hitter has seen four pitches. The more pitches a hitter sees, the more likely he is to make solid contact. Thus, 2-2 often requires a more precise pitch because the hitter has had a long look at the pitcher's offerings.

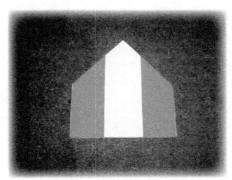

Pitch location = dark shade

Variation #4: "Strikeout" Fastball

Count used: 0-2. (Use in additional two-strike counts as situation dictates.)
  • 0-2 is the one chance a pitcher has to attempt to strike the hitter out. Anything can happen once the ball is put in play, and, on average, a quarter of balls put in play find a home – a hit or error. Even if the pitcher makes a great pitch and gets weak contact, he cannot protect against the blooper or swinging bunt. So, when 0-2, the pitcher is far enough ahead to safely attempt a strikeout. If he fails, he simply continues to work toward weak contact. Strikeouts are always outs (ignoring the drop third strike rule). Weak contact can have any number of outcomes.
  • Typical location: Just out of the strike zone, typically up, outside or inside.

The Changeup

Variation #1: "Called Strike" Changeup

Counts used: 0-0, 1-0, 2-1, 2-0, 3-1, 3-2
- The hitter never expects changeup when the pitcher is behind in the count, so the pitcher has tremendous room for error. Because the hitter is expecting fastball, even a mediocre changeup down the middle of the plate will be effective due to speed change and movement.
- Typical location: Down the middle

Variation #2: "Contact" Changeup

Counts used: 1-1, 1-2, 2-2
- The hitter is even or behind in these counts and has possibly seen a changeup at least once. Thus, we want the changeup to be down and toward the edges of the plate, ensuring weak contact.
- Typical location: Down, regardless of location. And on the halves or thirds of the plate, depending on movement.

Variation #3: "Strikeout" Changeup

Counts used: 0-2. (Use in additional two-strike counts as situation dictates.)
- This changeup needs to produce a strikeout. Again, in an 0-2 count, even weak contact is unacceptable. Strikeout or ball.
- Typical location: Starts at kneecap, ends up bouncing. Can be middle or on thirds of plate, as long as it ends up in or very near the dirt.

The Breaking Ball

Variation #1: "Called Strike" Breaking Ball

Counts used: 0-0, 1-0, 2-0, 2-1, 3-1, 3-2
- The ability to throw a breaking ball for a called strike is an important attribute separating elite pitchers from everyone else. Being able to throw a hard-biting pitch (remember – don't ease up on it) that breaks into the strike zone convinces the hitter to expect any pitch at any time.
- Typical location: Breaking into the heart of the strike zone, ideally between knee and mid-thigh height.

Variation #2: "Ahead in the Count" Breaking Ball

Counts used: 0-1, 1-1, 1-2
     • The 1-1 count is included here because it is a very high contact count, meaning hitters often swing on it and put the ball in play. Therefore, this pitch works best when it crosses farther away from mid-plate.
     • Typical location: Ending height between mid-shin and the knee on outside third of the plate.

Variation #3: "Strikeout" Breaking Ball

Counts used: 0-2. (Use in additional two-strike counts as situation dictates.)
     • This breaking ball starts as a low strike and breaks into the ground between the dirt in front of the plate and the point of the plate. It is unacceptable to throw a curve catchable in the air on an 0-2 count. Catchable with mitt on the dirt is OK.
     • Typical location: Starts as a strike, breaks out of the zone into the dirt and/or off the edge of the plate.

Discussion of the Above Recommendations

The Big Point: As you get strikes, move the ball farther away from mid-plate. This concept seems obvious, but many pitchers seem to have little to no grasp of it.

The pattern outlined above that applies to all of the pitch variations is very simple: as the pitcher gets further ahead in the count, he should move his pitches farther to the edges of the plate. The more work the pitcher has done to throw strikes early and get ahead, the harder it should become for the hitter to get a decent pitch to hit. Watch a big league game – what do they throw on 0-2 counts? It's almost always a fastball up or just off the plate or an offspeed pitch in the dirt; it rarely fails. Progressing toward the edges of the plate is what pitching is all about. Even if pitch selection is poor, as long as location is good, good things will happen. This is because the barrel of the bat lives in the middle of the plate. One of my favorite quotes is from coach Brooks Carey:

"The barrel is the shark; the end-cap and handle are minnows. The sharks swim in the middle of the plate; the minnows swim on the corners. You can swim with the minnows all day long, but don't you go swimming with the sharks…they bite."

However, as has been explained in numerous places in this book, none of these ideas are set in stone. Everything provided in this pitch sequence chapter is what makes sense most of the time. It never makes sense to throw a pitch right down the middle on 0-1, 1-2, or 0-2. It never makes sense to bounce a curveball on 3-0. However, throwing a changeup down in the zone on 3-2 might make sense, as might a curveball in the dirt on 1-1, or any number of scenarios.

There's a tremendous amount of variability in baseball requiring judgment made during the game that we can't predict here in conjecture. Maybe a hitter loves curveballs down the middle and looks for them – it wouldn't make sense to throw this hitter a curve down the middle in any count. Remember: we can apply generalizations to most situations, but the final call must be made according to the game situation and the pitcher's read on the individual hitter.

Expanding the Strike Zone

Consistently hitting a location is the best way to force both the hitter to swing at it and the umpire to call it. Pitchers who are all over the place but occasionally throw a beautiful pitch right on the black rarely get a strike call. But pitchers who consistently pound the middle, then the half, then the third, then finally the black of the plate, pulling the hitter and umpire out there, forcing swings and strike calls. After all, if a hitter will swing at a pitch one inch off the plate, why wouldn't he swing at a pitch two inches off? The best way to get more strike calls and swings at quality pitches is to simply throw more quality pitches.

Effective Pitch Velocity

This is a crucial concept to understand, as it refers to the way location, bat speed and pitch velocity interact to affect a hitter's ability to time a pitch. In essence, this hinges on two maxims:

1. To hit the ball hard, the hitter must get the barrel of his bat on the ball.
2. To do this, he must time his swing with both the speed of the pitch and its location.

The implications of these maxims:
  • To get the barrel on pitches on the inside of the plate, the hitter must swing earlier because the barrel of the bat must be in front of the plate to hit the ball squarely into fair territory. This effectively decreases bat speed because the hitter's bat must travel farther to meet a pitch on the inside part of the plate.
  • To get the barrel on pitches on the outside of the plate, the hitter can wait longer to swing because the barrel of the bat will be deeper on the plate when contact is made. This effectively increases bat speed because the hitter can catch up to a faster pitch on the out side part of the plate.
  • When hitters are behind in the count, they wait longer to swing, which effectively decreases bat speed.
  • When hitters are ahead in the count, they can be aggressive, which effectively increases bat speed.

- After seeing fastballs, hitters' timing mirrors the fastball velocity, effectively increasing bat speed.
- After seeing multiple offspeed pitches, timing mirrors the offspeed velocity, effectively decreasing bat speed.
- Decreased batspeed = increased effective pitch velocity.
- Increased batspeed = decreased effective pitch velocity.

Good pitch sequences follow the rules of effective velocity. Most pitchers have heard "hard in, soft away." This adage is a very simple summary of effective velocity, as throwing offspeed pitches away (soft) slows the hitters effective bat speed, making pitches in (hard) seem relatively faster and thus more difficult to catch up with.

Showing effective velocity for a left-handed hitter (left) and right-handed hitter (right).
Pitches on the inner half (light gray) seem faster to a hitter than pitches away (dark gray).

<u>The Rules of Pitch Sequencing</u>

Rule #1: Progressively move off of the plate.

As the pitcher throws strikes, he must make subsequent pitches harder to hit – the simplest way to do this is by moving their location farther away from the center of the plate. I discussed this above, but it needs to sink in – the more strikes gained on the hitter, the more the hitter should feel impending doom.

Pitch 1

Pitch 2

Pitch 3

Rule #2: Change speeds according to effective velocity.

Let the hitter's batspeed be the guide – by mixing pitches according to the maxims of effective velocity, timing will be optimally disrupted. Hard in, soft away; hard up, soft down.

Changing speeds is crucial to any pitcher's success, but the hitter's bat speed and timing needs to be the guide. A few ways of judging the hitter's bat speed include:

1. Spot in the batting order. Hitters 1-4 have the best bat speed; 7-9 have the worst; 5-6 are somewhere in between.
2. Foul balls. On a fastball thrown down the middle, does the hitter hit it up the middle, spray it foul the opposite way, or pull it foul? This will give clues about the hitter's bat speed, timing and tendencies. A foul ball straight back means the hitter is slightly late, not "right on" the pitch as some like to think.
3. Swing quality. Is the swing short and compact or long and loopy? Does the hitter step straight ahead, closed or way open? This will affect their ability to hit certain speeds and locations.

Above all, make a hitter prove he can hit the fastball before throwing him too much offspeed. Too many pitchers with good fastballs throw changeups to those who couldn't even catch up with a fastball.

Rule #3: Be predictable until it doesn't work.

Pitchers who have great offspeed pitches will typically throw them to get swings and misses later in the count; after all, why wouldn't they? If a pitcher has an incredible curveball and has a hitter 0-2…it makes good sense to throw a curveball.

But, if a pitcher throws a curveball every time he gets 0-2, hitters will start to catch on. But, if it works once, try it twice. If it works twice, try it thrice. If something is working, force the hitters to prove that it no longer works – many pitchers would be shocked at how stupid hitters can be, and how little they catch on to patterns. If a pattern works, stick with it until it's very obvious that it doesn't. If predictable is effective, then why bother being unpredictable?

Rule #4: Be wary of repeat at-bats.

Rule #3 states that we should stick with what works until the hitters adjust. Most hitters will start to catch on in the second and third time through the order. Bad hitters get themselves out on the same pitches; good hitters refuse to let pitchers get them out the same way twice. So, when hitters start coming up a second and third time, it's time to reevaluate strategy by asking a few questions:

- Are the hitters starting to take pitches that they swung at earlier?
- Are more balls being hit hard? If so, why?
- Are hitters starting to swing earlier?
- Are hitters taking big hacks at certain pitches (like they know what's coming)?

If the answers to the above are no....keep on dominating and don't change a thing. If "yes" pops up one or more times, it may be time to start changing the pattern by mixing up the counts in which one or more pitches are typically thrown.

Rule #5: Change and mirror eye level.

Hitters get comfortable when they know a pitcher is going to throw consistently into one part of the zone. They can then plant their feet and focus on a smaller area of the strike zone. Good pitchers will mix their fastball location to mirror both the starting and ending points of their breaking balls.

Curveball pitchers have an advantage because a high fastball will look like a curveball that drops in for a called strike. For these pitchers, when the hitter sees the ball going up, he won't know if it's a fastball or a curve for a strike; thus he is forced to swing at both pitches. Additionally, curveballs that break into the dirt start at the same point as fastballs thrown down the middle. Changing eye level with high effect is easy for these pitchers.

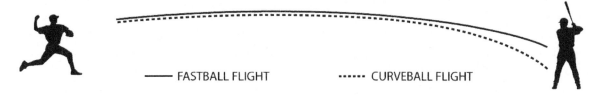

For those throwing predominantly changeups, sliders and sinkers, the fastball should stay down in the zone, where these three pitches break most sharply. Sliders and changeups that start high stay high, whereas curveballs can start high and break low. Thus, hitters know that when a slider/changeup/sinker pitcher leaves a ball up in the zone, it's going to be an easy pitch to hit. By keeping the fastball and offspeed arsenal down in the zone, all pitches will look similar out of the hand.

But, it's still a good idea to regularly change eye level at least some of the time. We never want to leave balls letters-high in the middle of the zone, but moving the ball up and in makes a big impact on a hitter's comfort level, as I will discuss below.

Rule #6: Be scary. Throw inside.

Hitters don't want to get hit in the face.

Commanding both the inside and outside of the plate is crucial to a pitcher's success. The outside corner gets a lot of press as being the most effective location, but when hitters consistently see it, they will start to cheat and lean over the plate. Throwing inside and outside keeps hitters honest and allows the pitcher to throw to all locations of the plate.

Additionally, throwing hard fastballs up and in, even ones that aren't strikes, is probably the single most effective thing a pitcher can do to "open up" the outer half of the plate.

Again, when pitchers are consistently throwing strikes, a hitter learns that he can be comfortable in the box because strikes aren't threatening his safety. Too many pitchers who are good at throwing strikes end up with little to no "presence" on the mound. Hitters need to know that they don't control the plate and aren't allowed to dive in and take big cuts at strikes. We keep these hitters in check by reminding them that if they aren't ready to move, they probably won't get out of the way in time.

Hitting batters is not necessary to be intimidating, nor is what I am advocating in this book. But I am advocating throwing hard fastballs inside from time to time to make sure hitters know they can't dig in, lean over the plate and expect to hit fastballs on the outside corner. Imagine if you were on deck, and the pitcher had just hit the previous two batters with 95-mph fastballs. How would you feel about getting in the box? Would you be eager to lean over the plate to shoot a changeup into the gap? I don't think so. Therefore, you as a fearful hitter would be less likely to hit a ball in the middle of the plate that normally might be easy to hit.

While throwing strikes is crucial, so is the occasional brush-back to make sure the hitter respects you. If he moves his feet after throwing inside, you've done your job and he won't dig in as confidently on the next pitch.

Rule #7: Double up.

Don't do this: Fastball. Curveball. Fastball. Curveball. Fastball.

A sequence like this one is ineffective and does nothing to alter the hitter's timing. Hitters adjust to speed the more they see it. A good example is early in the season – hitters struggle to hit good fastballs because they only saw BP speed during the offseason. Yet, the more they see it, the more their eyes adjust. The same happens in a microcosm during at-bats – hitters adjust to speeds when they see them over and over. So to best exploit and use effective velocity to ones advantage, we want to double up pitches more often. This isn't to say always double up; but, as a rule of thumb, know that if it's the right pitch call on one pitch, it's probably a still a good call on the next pitch.

Additionally, there's nothing more demoralizing for a hitter than a pitcher who throws two breaking balls in a row for strikes. The helpless look on a hitter's face after such a display of offspeed command is priceless.

A better sequence: Fastball. Fastball. Curveball. Curveball. Fastball. (Go sit down)

Rule #8: Misses are still effective.

Many pitchers make the mistake of thinking that when they throw offspeed pitches for balls, they don't fulfill their purpose; this isn't true. Any offspeed offering will affect the hitter's timing, though those thrown for strikes will have the greatest effect. Even if a pitcher misses with a few offerings, it's still setting him up to beat the hitter when he subsequently changes speeds.

Rule #9: Pitch to strengths first.

Say a hitter can't hit an inside fastball. Should the pitcher throw inside fastballs? Well, it depends on whether or not that inside pitch is a strength of the pitcher.

Scouting reports can lead pitchers astray when the focus turns to pitching to weaknesses instead of pitching off strengths. What if the scouting report said that a hitter can't hit lefties well? Should a righthander switch his glove and pitch with his left? We'd all agree – of course not.

So if a pitcher can't throw an inside fastball very well, it's simply not the right pitch to throw, regardless of the scouting report. Too many pitchers get beat throwing pitches they can't execute a high percentage of the time because they're trying to exploit a hitter's weakness. If the pitcher tries to go inside and misses (which he often will if it's a weakness), where will the miss be? Over the middle of the plate. What will happen to that pitch? Something bad.

It's better to pick and choose ones battles and stick with strengths. No hitter, especially at the amateur level, is without multiple weaknesses. So, it's easier to just keep searching for a weakness that is also a pitcher's strength. Plus, hitters get themselves out on easily hittable pitches all the time, so it's not necessary to attempt to shoot only for weaknesses.

Rule #10: Learn from it.

Great pitches will sometimes get clobbered; bad pitches often get popped up. There's never 100% certainty of any outcome, but it is important to analyze risk and reward and cause and effect. The best thing a pitcher can do is simply think hard about his pitch selection then remember what happens. Every pitcher will select pitches according to his strengths and weaknesses, style of pitching, level of courage, aggression, etc. What matters most is that there's a good reason behind a pitch call. If there is, then no second-guessing is necessary, even if he decides he might not throw that same pitch again.

Rule #11: Force hitters to repeat bad swings.

If a hitter swings very late on a fastball, throw it by him a second time. And, if he swings late at that one, throw it by him a third time. If a hitter takes an atrocious swing on a curveball, throw it again – exploit his ugly swings. When hitters take bad swings, it's a good sign that they struggle with that pitch in that location. So, don't do them any favors by switching to pitches that they might be more comfortable with – make them repeat their ugliest swing. Once you see them start to adjust, then move on to other locations and pitch selections.

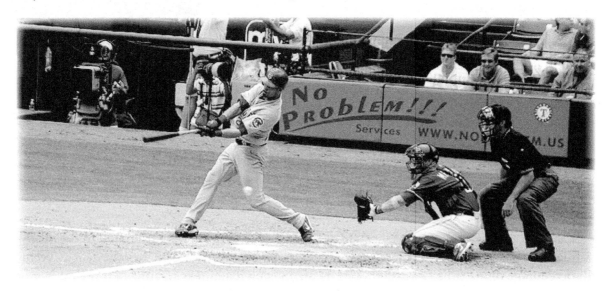

Rule #12: If they're down, keep them down.

The last thing a pitcher wants to do is get from 0-2 back to 2-2 or 3-2. If you're ahead in the count, force the hitter to swing while he is disadvantaged. While we don't want to leave the ball down the middle of the plate, we still want to be aggressive with offerings – pitches that will entice swings. Common, faulty wisdom is to "waste" the 0-2 pitch; we don't want this. What we want is a ball that looks like a strike on 0-2, and a very difficult to hit strike on 1-2. Many pitchers get too fine on 0-2 and 1-2 and end up throwing pitches that never have a chance to be a strike, and thus quickly find themselves back in even counts. Attack and force them to swing while they're down.

FAQ – *Should I "waste" a pitch on 0-2? I don't want to give up a hit.*

No. Let's think about this:

0-2 is the most advantageous count. "Wasting" a pitch implies throwing a useless pitch to move the count to 1-2. We want the hitter to do one of two things on 0-2: strike out or take the pitch for a ball. Because the goal on 0-2 is to get a strikeout, thus ensuring that the batter will not reach base by hit, error or fielder's choice, we must throw a pitch that appears to be a strike but ends up an unhittable ball. If we throw this pitch correctly, the hitter should not be able to even make contact – foul or otherwise. So, if he swings, he strikes out; if he takes, he gets to 1-2. Wasting a pitch is the wrong term – we want to throw a zero-sum pitch – strikeout or ball; nothing in between. And, we need to still be efficient with pitch counts, so getting a hitter out on the minimum number of pitches should always be the goal – 0-2 strikeouts require 25% fewer pitches than 1-2 strikeouts.

CHAPTER 11

SITUATIONAL PITCHING

Understanding when to be more aggressive with offspeed pitches, when to pitch for contact and when to look to a strikeout can save a pitcher runs and wins. Pitching to the score, ending two-out innings as quickly as possible, preventing manufactured runs, knowing the batting order and pitching to preserve momentum all play a huge role in a pitcher's effectiveness.

Baseball is a game of constant risk and reward that changes according to the count, the score, the inning and the amount of runners on base. Learning to pitch effectively to the situation is a skill that comes with experience and confidence, but having a good understanding of how risk and reward changes will steer an inexperienced pitcher in the right direction.

Situational Pitching Maxim #1: Get back in the dugout.

Pitching is much like golf – the less you play, the better you play. Golfers want fewer strokes, and pitchers need to throw fewer pitches and face fewer hitters. Regardless of the situation, efficiency and getting hitters out quickly must be the number one goal.

A common mistake inexperienced pitchers make is getting too fancy with two outs. While legitimate two-out rallies happen, they're rare – other than a homerun, it takes at least two base runners to manufacture just one run, and hitters are generally demoralized when coming to the plate with two outs, especially when the bases are empty.

A "shut-down mentality" is what a pitcher needs when he already has two outs. His game plan should be to more aggressively attack the strike zone, which usually means more fastballs in fastball counts and going after the white of the plate. Assuming a pitcher doesn't walk anyone, to score a run it will take three consecutive singles without another out – an unlikely outcome regardless of the game situation.

Nothing frustrates managers, scouts and teammates more than a pitcher who gets two quick outs just to start walking hitters. Once two outs are recorded, the inning must be completed as quickly as possible. Get back in the dugout as fast as you can.

Situational Pitching Maxim #2: Pitch to the score.

Way Ahead

If your team has a lead of five runs or more, it's unlikely that your opponent will bat in enough runs to catch up without the aid of walks. If your team has a large lead, it means two things – your team has hot bats and their team has "mop-up" pitchers in the game. So, it's safe to assume a big lead will continue to grow.

The pitcher's job when given a large lead is to force hitters to earn their way on base. While this is always the pitcher's job, it becomes paramount with a lead. This is because a team that's down is unlikely to string together the 10 or so hits required to score five or more runs. But, four walks and six hits will do the job just the same with much less effort. Most big leads form and evaporate

150

because a pitcher is doing a combination of bad things – walking batters and giving up hits. It's rare that a pitcher will give up six runs on zero walks.

"Having good coverage

Way Behind

This is the time to prove your worth to a team and be tough for them. The only way to come back from a deficit is to stop the opposing team's momentum while building your own offensive momentum. Typically, as discussed in the previous paragraph, your team has given up a large amount of runs because of control problems – walks and hit batters plus hits. So, the first thing a team needs from a "mop-up" pitcher is strikes. Throw strikes and stop giving the opposition free bases, from which only one or two hits will score runs.

Most games get out of hand because when a pitcher gives up a handful of runs, he mentally gives up. This allows the floodgates to open. But, the "chip away" mentality is the only way to get back into a game – throw quality innings while hoping the offense can provide a run or two per inning.

Close Game

This one doesn't require much explication – if the game is tight, make good pitches and battle your opponents. May the best man win.

Situational Pitching Maxim #3: Make them earn a manufactured run.

In certain situations, a batter can help score a run by simply putting the ball in play without a base hit. No hitter executes these manufactured situations perfectly every single time, so an intelligent pitcher can maximize his chances of preventing the hitter from succeeding at what is usually a somewhat easy job.

Runner on Second with Zero Outs

What the hitter wants to do: Place a ground ball to the right side.

This is simple baseball – with a runner on second and nobody out, a ground ball to the right side is the easiest solution to advance the runner to third. Once on third, the runner will score on a ground ball to the middle infield (provided they play back) or a sacrifice fly.

151

So, screw him – let's make that job difficult.

What the pitcher wants to do: Get a grounder to the left side (among other things such as
a pop-up or strikeout)

If the hitter is a righty, the solution is simple – pound the ball inside. How is a right-handed hitter going to hit a ground ball to the second baseman on a fastball at his fists? The answer is that he's not. Pitching a righthanded hitter inside will make it virtually impossible for him to do anything but pull the ball or hit a weak, fisted grounder back to the pitcher. Good fastballs inside are also tough to lift, so a deep fly ball won't be happening, either.

A good breaking ball or changeup down in the zone, especially after some hard fastballs in, will also be a good choice – a hitter out on his front foot trying to hit a pitch down in the zone will typically hit a roll-over grounder, which for the righty goes to the left side of the infield, preventing the runner's advancement.

If the hitter is a lefty, his job is super easy – he just has to roll over on a ground ball. So, pitches down in the zone won't work as well, because if he gets any piece of a nice breaking ball, it's probably going to the right side of the infield. But, the solution is still straightforward – pound the ball away, forcing him to pull an outside pitch if he wants to advance the runner. Lefties naturally like to pull a bit more than righties, so it'll take a good approach for him to get the job done on any pitch located on the outside third of the plate.

Runner on Third with One or No Outs – Infield In

What the hitter wants to do: Lift the ball deep into the outfield.
What the pitcher wants to do: Keep the ball on the ground.

Righty or lefty hitters get the same dose in this situation – fastballs tightly in. The goal with the infield in is, well, to keep the ball on the infield. If the pitcher gets a ground ball to an infielder, the runner either has to hold or is cut down at the plate.

The ball is most easily lifted when the hitter can extend his arms, and when there is air beneath the pitch. So, our two points of attack are inside below the hands or down – two locations more likely to produce a grounder.

It's also crucial in this situation to understand the implications on pitch selection. If the infield is drawn in, it means the potential run on third base is important. So, everyones mindset must be: don't let that runner score. While no pitcher wants any runner to score, this situation is different. What's different is that pitch selection can be less conservative with regard to location and pitch selection. The salient feature is that there's an open base behind the lead runner, so walking the hitter isn't much of a bother.

152

In an ordinary 2-0 count, for example, it usually makes sense to go with the high-percentage strike pitch, the fastball, even though the hitter also expects it. But with an important run at third and with first base open, there's little harm done if the pitcher walks the hitter while trying to throw more offspeed pitches in fastball counts. In this situation, we only care about the runner on third. So, we can try extra hard to get the hitter out by throwing pitches we might not normally throw (again – offspeed stuff when behind in the count, or strikeout pitches in any two-strike count) to try to keep that run from scoring. And what happens if we walk that hitter? We have first and third, can allow the middle infield to play for a double play ball that will end the inning if there's one out. Or, if there's no one out and the infield stays in, big deal – we still only care about the runner on third.

But, regardless of pitch selection, location is still king. If the pitch goes up, the hitter is simply going to toss his bat at it; up into the outfield it will go, and the runner will score.

Runner on Third with One or No Outs – Infield Back

What the hitter wants to do: Lift the ball deep or hit a middle grounder.
What the pitcher wants to do: Get a grounder to a corner infielder.

In all of the situations presented in this chapter, we know that more than just a ground ball will get the desired result. Strikeouts are huge with runners on base, and pop-ups to the infield keep everyone at bay. But, we have to first get to two strikes to even think about strikeout strategy, so the scope of this chapter is more of the initial at-bat approach. If the pre-pitch mindset is, "Get a ground ball to the third baseman!" – great, we have a plan. And if, while executing that plan, we get to two strikes, even better – now the plan can change to "Screw this guy, I'm striking him out!"

With a runner on third and less than two outs, the infield will typically play back to trade an out for a run. They will do this in non-critical situations such as the third inning or when one team or the other has a decent lead and wants to avoid a big inning. Trading the run for an out with a runner on third means that a rally basically ends once the bases clear.

So, a grounder up the middle is going to be fielded by the shortstop or second baseman and thrown to first. To avoid giving up a run in this situation, the ball must be directed to one of three players who will go to the plate if the ball is hit sharply to them – the pitcher, first baseman and third baseman.

The strategy for this situation is similar to the others – pick a side of the plate and force the batter to either yank an outside pitch up the middle or get his hands in fast enough to barrel up an inside pitch to the middle of the yard. If a pitcher hits his spots on the thirds of the plate, it won't be easy for the hitter to punch one up the middle. But, realistically, it's not easy to ensure that he hits the ball to a corner infielder, either. The goal is to simply have a plan, attack it, and hope for the best.

Additionally, any situation with first base open gives the pitcher a chance to exploit a hitter a little more than normal. If a hitter has proven he struggles with breaking balls, throw him a few more than normal – make him really earn that RBI. With a base open, you can bounce a few more sliders, curves or changeups trying to get that swing and miss. You can treat a 1-2 or 2-2 count like 0-2 when there is a base open behind a lead runner.

Bases Loaded

Pitching with the bases loaded is especially difficult for three reasons:
1. A walk forces in a run, so strikes must be thrown.
2. Pitching inside leaves less room for error – a hit batsman results in a run.
3. It's scary to throw strikes because a hit scores multiple runs.

The one-pitch-at-a-time mentality is especially crucial with the bases loaded. With so many possible negative outcomes, the way out of trouble often seems impossibly long and difficult; it's easy to get frustrated. The fact remains that pitching with the bases loaded should be internalized the same as any other situation – the pitcher needs to simply make one quality pitch at a time.

Any time the bases are loaded with no one out, the goal is simple: damage control. Escaping this situation with two or fewer runs scored is a good outcome. When one or no runs score, the pitcher deserves a big pat on the back.

Games are often won or lost based on one big inning rather than many one-run innings. So, when a pitcher finds himself with the bases loaded and no outs, he first must think about getting an out, which, again, starts with a quality strike. Falling behind in the count means a pitcher must come up with fastballs when a hitter is more than willing to take a homerun hack in hopes of being a hero. A 2-0 count with the bases loaded is the worst possible place for a pitcher to be.

The Quickest Route Out

With no outs, the fastest path out of the inning with no runs scoring is a strikeout and a double play. So, the pitcher must pave this path by starting off the at-bat with strike one. If he can get to two strikes, he must possess a razor-sharp focus to make a great strikeout pitch. If the strikeout can be made, help is on the way – quality pitches down in the zone and to the thirds of the plate will produce ground balls. A hard ground ball on the infield can produce that double play that quickly ends the bases-loaded threat.

But, getting out of the jam with zero runs isn't realistic most of the time, and surrendering one or fewer is a job well done in damage control. It starts with quality strikes in hopes of inducing ground balls.

General Bunt Situations

Pitchers sometimes get themselves in trouble trying to prevent bunts. A bunt is a free out – take it. But if a pitcher has solid command and wishes to make life difficult on the bunter, he can do a few things:
1. Brush him back.
2. Throw in tight.
3. Throw a strikeout breaking ball.

Hitters don't like getting hit in the face.

I know that statement continues to be shocking, but it's true – most hitters will avoid putting their moneymaker in harm's way. So, if a pitcher is confident in his ability to come back with strikes and not walk the hitter, he can certainly throw one up and in to scare the would-be bunter. Few hitters, after being brushed back, will boldly put their faces down by the plate to poke that outside fastball. Is this a waste pitch (which I said didn't exist earlier)? Not exactly – it's a purpose pitch in that it can accomplish a major task – reduce likelihood of a subsequent bunt attempt. Plus, if the hitter attempts to bunt a brush-back, he'll pop it up or at least be down 0-1.

Beyond the purely purposed brush-back pitch, it is difficult to bunt balls thrown close to the body. Pitching inside to a hitter who is squaring to bunt will make it tough for him to both square the pitch up and avoid being hit simultaneously.

Fastballs inside and up are difficult to bunt, as are breaking balls thrown down in the zone. It's important to understand, though, that the goal of a bunter is to place the ball on the ground. A breaking ball breaks downward, so when thrown over the plate, this downward break can aid the bunter in keeping it out of the air. So, throwing breaking balls for strikes isn't a great idea, but throwing them for a strikeout (bouncing on the plate) will force the hitter to lunge and stab at the ball, resulting in misses. If the hitter gets down in the count while trying to bunt, a good strikeout breaking ball can be a great way to get the punch out and prevent advancement of the runner.

Directional Bunts

In many cases, a hitter will need to bunt to one foul line or the other to ensure the lead runner can advance without being cut down by a well-placed fielder. Depending on the situation, either the first or third baseman will be available to sprint in and not worry about covering a base. Because of this, the bunter will attempt to avoid bunting in that direction.

An example: with a runner on second base with zero outs, a team tries to sacrifice the runner to third. The first baseman has no runner to hold, so he plays very close to the plate and sprints even closer when the hitter squares to bunt. If the hitter bunts to the first base side, the ball will be quickly fielded and the runner will likely be thrown out at third. So, the hitter is expected to bunt to the third base side to ensure the runner can advance. The third baseman must stay at the base to receive the throw, leaving the pitcher to field a bunt to that side. In this situation, we have the following breakdown:

What the hitter wants to do: Bunt to third base.
What the pitcher wants to do: Induce a bunt to first base.

As we previously discussed, the solution to this problem is straightforward: throw pitches to the side of the plate that we want the ball to go. If the pitcher wants the hitter to bunt to the right side, he should throw to that side of the plate – it's tough for the hitter to get his bat around the pitch to bunt it the other way. Regardless of the situation, if it's clear a directional bunt is needed, pitch to a location that makes executing that direction difficult.

Situational Pitching Maxim #4: Pitch to who's up, who's on deck, and who's on base.

You see this in the Major Leagues all the time: The pitcher's spot is up next with two outs and a base open; what does the team do? They walk the 8-hole hitter to bring the pitcher up. While an extreme example, this makes sense – why bother taking a risk with a relatively weaker hitter is on deck? This is called "pitching around a hitter," and it's a very important concept. It rarely means walking him intentionally – it usually means throwing filthy pitches at very precise locations so that only one of two things will happen: if he swings at it, he's going to make poor contact, and if he takes it'll either be a ball or a tough strike.

The salient feature is having a base open. If first base is unoccupied with a lead runner on second or third, there's little harm in walking a batter, especially with two outs. With two outs and no one on base, it's best to take chances with whoever might be up, because they can't do much damage with empty bases. Understand, though: We don't just walk the hitter, we just choose pitches that are both more difficult to throw and more difficult to hit. This might mean throwing a 2-0 slider or a 1-1 changeup on the corner of the plate. Because the base is open, we can take chances throwing pitches difficult to hit for even the oppositions best hitter. There's no reason to throw a 2-0 fastball down the middle when there's a place to put him.

The applications of this stem from a few qualities of the hitter on deck:
   1. His skill – How good is he?
   2. His day – how is he hitting today?
   3. His handedness –lefty or righty?

Some pitchers are better at matching their armside with the hitter – you see MLB managers looking for lefty-lefty pitching matchups all the time. If a pitcher is a lefty and a lefty is on deck, he might pitch around the righty at the plate because he's more likely to get an out against the guy on deck.

If a hot hitter is at the plate, they might pitch around him to get to the relatively colder hitter on deck. If the guy up has hit two doubles in two at-bats, whereas the on-deck hitter is 0-for-2 with two pop-ups, it's obviously better to pitch to the guy who's struggling. And if the hitter is just really good in general, regardless of his previous at-bats, he's always a possible candidate for a pitch-around. Sensible pitch calls take into account the skill of the hitter and the pitcher's likelihood to get him out.

All of this is simple risk vs. reward. With a runner on second or third and first unoccupied, the risk involved in issuing a walk drops dramatically – the lead runner does not advance, the double play becomes in order, and no runs are forced in. This allows a pitcher to pitch around a hitter if he chooses it prudent, based on the skill of the hitter who's up relative to who's on deck.

Situational Pitching Maxim #5: Ride the Momentum Wave.

Say your team just got you the lead with a nice rally. Or, maybe they battled to close a big gap and tighten the game. What's the worst thing a pitcher can do in the inning that follows? Walk the leadoff hitter.

The best pitchers feed off momentum and do their part to continue a rally. A rally is not just a collection of runs, but a collection of energy gained by a team when innings are successful. A successful offensive inning must be continued by a successful defensive inning to keep the rally alive. And, the sooner your hitters get back to the plate, the greater the chance of continuing the rally.

When a pitcher's team provides him with precious runs, he must get excited, focused, and run out the mound to keep the knife pressed to the other team's throat, so to speak. The entire game can shift when a team's offense grabs three runs and its pitcher responds with a 1-2-3 inning.

While a pitcher can't control what happens after he releases a pitch, he has full control over his focus and approach before the pitch. Focused pitchers, while riding a rally, will attack the strike zone and aggressively pursue outs.

CHAPTER 12
MENTAL TRAINING GUIDELINES

It's a common misconception that good pitching mechanics must produce good control; this isn't always the case. When pitchers with good, repeatable mechanics struggle to find the zone, the cause of this trouble is rarely physical. There's a simple test to see if the mind is the weak link: compare bullpen accuracy to in-game accuracy. If a pitcher can throw strikes consistently in the bullpen, but not once inserted into a game, there's only one variable at play – the mind. The fear of getting hit hard, giving up runs and being embarrassed on the mound hinders the control and aggressiveness of nearly all pitchers. Those who succeed are the ones who learn to manage or eliminate these fears.

Additionally, it should be every athlete's goal to reduce game-induced stress, anxiety and negative thinking. To perform at the highest level possible, ones mindset must protect the individual against fear, stress, anxiety, pressure, inconsistency and unknown variables.

Mental Traits of Effective Pitchers

#1: Aggressive

The pitcher must throw strikes. Consistently walking hitters is a sure path to destruction. Good pitchers aggressively attack the strike zone without fear of the results. If a pitcher becomes obsessed with what might happen when he throws a pitch over the plate, crippling anxiety will ensue. The reality is that even good hitters often miss very hittable pitches. The pitcher needs to remain aggressive at all times and force the hitter to react to him, not vice versa.

#2: Combative

Being combative means having a competitive attitude toward the hitter. The hitter is largely irrelevant, the pitch must be thrown to the desired location regardless of what the hitter chooses to do with it. Yet, pitchers throw better with disdain and anger toward the opposing team. When a pitcher is prepared to fight, he will subsequently find himself inflating his own ego and finding fault in his opponent. This builds confidence, and confidence wins.

#3: Reassuring

I could use the term "confident," but it is overly broad. Pitchers who are reassuring remind themselves in times of duress and poor performance that they're still great, still capable, and still have better days ahead of them. When something goes wrong, they don't worry; they ride out the storm because they know the boat can't possibly sink.

#4: Forgetful

It's a timeless adage that baseball players must have short memories; it's true. A pitcher will throw countless pitches, innings and games in his career. If he's lucky, he will give up thousands of hits before retiring (a sign of a long career!). Those distraught and discouraged with poor results often let one bad pitch or at-bat ruin the rest of a game, one bad game ruin a week, and a bad week ruin a month. Those who can quickly shake off failure give themselves the best possible chance for future success.

#5: Observant

Learning the nuances of baseball is as simple as paying attention. The best players pay attention whether in the game or the dugout and constantly assess risk and reward, cause and effect, and the habits of other players. Too many pitchers don't pick up on hitters' habits, nor learn pitch sequencing or situational pitching because they're not engaged with the game. Because a pitcher will only pitch, on average, 5-15% of his team's total innings, it's important that he pay attention to the game the other 90% of the time; most of the learning will take place when not on the mound.

#6: Analytical

"I threw this pitch and that happened."

"I missed that spot because my mechanics did this…"

The best pitchers are their own pitching coaches, constantly assessing why they succeed, why they fail and how to make adjustments along the way. When one is observant, he sets the stage for self-analysis, and self-analysis leads to self-discovery.

#7: Arrogant

The time to be humble is after the game, when the job is done. Before the game, arrogance needs to be the prevalent attitude – are you better than your competition?

"You're darn right I am – by a long shot. This team has no chance of even sniffing the baseball today. Runs? They'll be lucky to get a single hit. Even on my bad days I'm unhittable."

There's no room for doubt, humility or second-guessing. You're the best there's ever been. Period. If they get a hit, it's a fluke. If they get a bunch of hits, wow – they won the lottery.

#8: Unfettered

To be unfettered means being confident, focused and undeterred in the face of adversity. Pitchers will find themselves in the most stressful situations of any player – one pitch can, and often does, determine the outcome of the entire game. Bases loaded with no outs? Winning run on third? A 3-1 count on the cleanup hitter? Thousands in the crowd screaming against you? Hecklers in your ear? Great pitchers learn not only to remain calm, but to thrive amid pressure and distraction.

#9: Disconnected

After a bad performance, a pitcher often has multiple days until he gets a chance to rectify it. Dwelling on a poor outing will only cause more stress and anxiety the next time out. It's important to separate oneself from baseball when off the field, for the sake of personal happiness. Your personal life should never suffer because of a bad game, and baseball will stay fun and exciting if two separate lives are lived.

#10: Consistent

Routine is important, and developing one requires a pitcher with a focus on organization – arranging his life in a structured manner to ensure consistency. The best pitchers learn what works for them, develop a plan around it, and then stick to it every time. Regardless of the between-game and pre-game ritual, the best pitchers adhere to them because consistency eliminates variables that might have a negative effect.

#11: Myopic

Myopic means near-sighted. It's demoralizing to think that every time a starting pitcher goes out to the mound, he's expected to complete seven innings while surrendering three runs or less. It seems an impossible task to think that one could throw a shutout – nine innings with no runs – or an even bigger task: a no hitter or perfect game. But, these good performances happen, and pitchers churn out great ERAs over long seasons. They do so by breaking games into small chunks.

It's seemingly impossible to get 27 hitters out in a row without allowing a base runner. But, is it possible to get through one perfect inning? Sure. Better yet: get one hitter out? Definitely. Even smaller: make one good pitch? Absolutely.

A perfect game is composed of nine innings, which we can subdivide into nine one-inning challenges. Each inning requires only three outs. Each out only requires, on average, four good pitches. Four good pitches are made one at a time, and so we arrive at the smallest unit in baseball: the pitch.

What we want is a one-pitch mindset. Make one perfect pitch. Then when that's complete, make one more perfect pitch. When all is said and done, a perfect game is thrown one pitch at a time. Breaking the game into manageable chunks will make it seem easy.

"I can make one great pitch. If I do that over and over, I'll have pitched a great game."

Easy.

Creating and Enhancing Positive Mental Traits

Positive Self-Talk

This is exactly what it sounds like: talking to yourself with words of encouragement and positivity. Confidence stems not only from past experiences of success but also self-worth. If others tell you that you're good, you'll believe it. And, if you can reassure yourself, you'll believe that too.

"You're the best. No can touch you when you're on the mound."

"You dominated last inning. Keep it up. One pitch at a time. They can't hit that slider."

"That last hitter was a fluke. They can't hit you. Keep doing what you're doing."

Positive Comparison

Positive comparison entails finding a player better than you, such as a Major Leaguer, and expounding upon similarities. An example:

"I have a great curveball and really good control. Cole Hamels also has a nasty curve and can throw the ball anywhere he wants, any time he wants. If Cole Hamels pitched today against this team, he'd probably throw a no-hitter with 20 strikeouts. I'm a lot like Cole Hamels; chances are pretty good I'll throw a no-hitter today."

It doesn't matter how accurate the comparison is – grab any common thread and pull on it – it will inspire confidence in a good outcome.

Trading Places

Another effective mental technique to boost confidence is visualizing the opposition, the fans, coaches and announcers talking positively about you. Say you have a 2.00 ERA and are 4-0. The opposing pitcher has an ERA of 5.50 and is 1-3. Who are others expecting to win the game? You, of course – the pitcher with the sterling ERA and win-loss record.

In this scenario, everyone on the opposition and in the stands would be talking about how tough a pitcher you were, how tough the game would be for your opposition, and how unlikely it is that you would be beaten. If you heard them say these things, wouldn't it make you feel powerful and confident? Absolutely it would. Well, chances are that people are saying those things. So, picture yourself outside, in the stands or in the dugout and visualize what they'd be saying about you. Picture the opposing players groaning about seeing your name on the lineup card. Picture the hitters rolling their eyes as they begrudgingly walk up to bat and admit defeat after you strike them out.

Even if your numbers aren't great, you have qualities that make you a sleeper, right? So, picture yourself next to a parent in the stands who knows how good you can be. If you're getting innings for a team, it means that they believe you have enough good qualities to do the job.

Listen in on those conversations:

"Yeah, his ERA isn't great, but he's just one start away from turning it around. His changeup is really filthy when it's on, and I've got a feeling it will be there today. The other team is going to really have their hands full if they take this game for granted."

Whatever you think your positive qualities and best abilities are, picture other people talking about them.

Meditation & Visualization

Meditation is the best means with which to change ones psyche. Every pitcher can benefit from it because it allows the pitcher to practice developing an optimal mental state. An optimal mental state for many will be one of relaxed, confident aggression, but is different for everyone.

To meditate, all one needs is a relaxing, quiet place and twenty minutes of time.

I suggest the following:
- Start at a time when you don't have to rush to finish. If you want to meditate for 20 minutes, give yourself 40 before having anything to do or anywhere to be.
- Lay on your back on the floor or sit upright on a soft cushion – being comfortable will prevent your body from aching and cramping, which will detract from the experience
- Focus on relaxing first. Let the shoulder blades melt into the floor.
- Utilize a belly breath – breathing with the stomach moving in and out boosts relaxation and oxygen uptake.
- Count the breaths. This is a great beginning technique to keep extraneous thoughts at bay.
- Realize that being antsy, bored and generally uncomfortable at first is normal. Trust us and keep going – ride it out and the feeling will fade in a week.

Meditation is highly personal and infinitely customizable. The biggest piece of the puzzle is learning to become comfortable doing nothing. Most people at first feel like they have to get up and do something, that they literally cannot meditate. But, after forcing themselves to do it consistently for just a few days, the anxiety starts to subside, replaced by a much broader feeling of relaxation and wellbeing.

Staying Present

The first task in a meditation practice is learning to become quiet with the mind, in a state that I refer to as present. Being present means staying focused on what's here right now, ignoring what happened in the past and what might happen in the future. For a pitcher, being present means being fixated on *this* pitch. The previous pitch is irrelevant, and the next pitch is irrelevant; all that matters is this one right now. Execute in the present without heeding anything else.

The best way to learn to stay present is by counting the breath. If we're living, we're breathing, so the breath will obviously follow us onto the mound. Because one cannot breathe in the past or the future, turning the focus to the breath can serve as a home base to get the mind off of distractions. Most, if not all, distractions in baseball are caused by negative outcomes that just happened (giving up a home run) or might happen (the winning run is on third, or a scout is watching in the stands).

When we count the breath, we learn to return our minds to that which is inherently present. When we focus on being present, all that which attempts to distract us from the past and future cannot take hold. And, because belly breaths help calm the physical body, we can utilize them during competition to help return us to a calm, relaxed state when the game gets stressful.

The Mind-Body Connection

We all remember our best games – we pick a pitch, throw it flawlessly, grab the ball again and repeat. We can barely recall any thoughts, any fans screaming, any wind, sun, rain or other distractions; everything just flows. This state of being "in the zone" is a meditative state – when we make one movement followed by another with no mental stoppage time, we're in a perfect balance of mind and body. Ideally, the mind gives the body a command, and the body, without inhibition, acts on it. This connection gets disrupted, though, by doubts, fear, and negativity.

"You're not good enough."

"He hit a bomb off you last time."

"If you don't throw well, that scout won't sign you."

"This is a big game; everyone is counting on you."

All of these doubts and negative thoughts cause the body anxiety and tension. The apprehension felt by the mind is transmitted to the muscles, preventing them from performing their task as they naturally would. By heeding negative thoughts in the mind, the physical body cannot perform at its full capacity.

The way we take the power back and be rid ourselves of negative thought is not by eliminating it; we will always have doubt and discouragement flowing through our minds. What we do is let it pass through unnoticed. Sure, the doubt still enters the mind, but we ignore it like a crying child – if we pay it no attention, over time it blends into the background as white noise, with no message and no ability to deter us. Listen to ten people talk at once and what do you hear? Nothing but noise; no specifics, no words and no phrases. We build our shield of armor against negativity and doubt by staying present and building confidence through experience, positive visualization, positive self-talk and positive comparison.

Clearing the Canvas

Mental training master Alan Jaeger, in a meditation seminar, gave the analogy of a television set to illustrate how meditation paves the way for visualization. Imagine a person painted a white X across the center of a TV screen. With the television turned on, the background of the television program would make focusing on the X very difficult. Yet, if one were to turn the TV off, the blackness of the set would suddenly make the white X pop out in great clarity. The mind is this same way – if we wanted to visualize ourselves performing well on the baseball field, or in any other aspect of life, the images would be much clearer without the background noise clouding the picture. Background noise in our minds consists of random thoughts as well as doubts and negative thoughts, both of which are very destructive to our physical abilities and confidence.

Visualization

Once we learn to meditate in a relaxed, comfortable state and stay present, we become more capable of visualization. When we have cleared our canvas, so to speak, we can start to place ourselves in stressful positions. While in the relaxed, comfortable state of meditation, entering a stressful situation becomes much easier. Picture yourself in a bases-loaded situation with no outs. How will you get out of it? Well, when visualizing the situation, you pick the pitches, pick the outcomes, pick your psyche and paint the rest of the picture. You can watch yourself dissect a hitter for a quick strikeout, followed by the magical 6-4-3 double play induced by an amazing curveball. Because it's all up to you, in your head, you can make yourself look heroic every time out.

These visualization sessions begin to seem very real, to the point where physical effects can actually be felt. A common situation of anxiety is throwing an offspeed pitch when behind in the count. When calling a 3-1 changeup in a meditation session, the body may tense up, if ever so slightly. Then, once the pitcher consistently sees himself succeeding throwing that 3-1 changeup, he will start to feel relaxed instead of anxious – he learns that he can do it. Then, when he finds himself in that same situation in a real game, he will associate those feelings of relaxation while meditating on those 3-1 changeups. And, if he doesn't, all he has to do is take a belly breath and return himself to the present. Visualization gives the pitcher the ability to practice his mental state while not in competition.

Bringing it All Together

Meditation can have a profound effect on any person, athlete or otherwise, by fostering feelings of relaxation and serenity amid stress. But, like any other skill, mental training takes practice. A daily meditation practice is needed to make permanent changes, but it requires only 20 minutes of time. Everyone has 20 minutes to spare – it's only a matter of whether they take mental training as seriously as physical training. To start a meditation practice, one needs to perform the following:

1. Set aside a 25-40-minute window in which to meditate
2. Find a quiet place to lay or sit comfortably
3. Relax. Let the body go completely limp
4. Belly breathe and count breaths
5. Allow the mind to relax and go any place it likes
6. If the mind is cluttered, counting the breaths will help to clear it
7. Once relatively clear, start a visualization that fosters a change you want to make
8. Hone in on details and make the situation as real as possible

Creating a Routine

A routine is very important. Doing the same things on game day keeps extraneous variables from getting in the way of your success.

Your routine is highly personal, so it would be difficult to define guidelines. But, a good routine before taking the mound on game day, whether as a starter or reliever, entails some of the following elements:

1. Physical preparedness
2. Reflection and meditation time
3. Consistent food and drink
4. Superstitions, if necessary

It's easiest to give an example. Here's the routine I followed as a starter in professional baseball, assuming a 7:05pm game time with 5:30pm report time.

10:00am: Awaken, stretch out the whole body and throwing arm before breakfast.

10:30am: Light breakfast consisting of water, coffee, protein shake and fruit.

10:30-1:00pm: Catch up on emails, phone calls, TV, reading, homework or business.

1:00pm:	Eat lunch – plenty of water, fruit, veggies, meat and nuts. This was my final big meal, as I never felt like eating too much before my starts.
2:00-3:00pm:	Meditate for 60 minutes. This was crucial to getting relaxed and preparing myself for the task at hand. I would review information on the team I was facing and my game plan, visualizing myself executing flawlessly and confidently.
3:00-4:30pm:	I would start to get antsy, and would generally just kill time before leaving for the field. I'd usually stretch my hips and shoulder a second time. I'd sometimes read, watch TV or a movie, go to a movie theater by myself occasionally, or just sort of space out around the house.
4:30-5:15pm:	I'd typically arrive at the field earlier than necessary and maybe catch the last few rounds of batting practice to cure my nervous boredom.
5:15-5:35pm:	Meditate for 20 minutes. This was my final preparation and a more aggressive meditation. This would leave me feeling passionate, excited and focused about destroying the opposing team. This was a very vivid meditation because of the clarity gained by my earlier meditation session.
5:35-6:00pm:	I'd very slowly and meticulously put on my uniform. I liked to take my time and not feel rushed. I'd then stare at my cleats for 5-10 minutes in a sort of meditation before heading to the training room to stretch.
6:00-6:15pm:	Quick stretch in the training room to get blood flowing. Headphones would be on, blasting aggressive music. Street Sweeper Social Club, Rage Against the Machine, Korn, Chevelle, Fort Minor, Three Days Grace and Metallica were common choices.
6:15pm:	Head out to the field. I would sit on the grass, headphones on, soak up the sun for a few minutes and get some last stretches in.
6:30pm:	Start moving. My warm up routine consisted of the following: • 2-poles hard jog • Walking high knees, hamstring kicks, lunges, drop lunges, side shuffles, power skips, tempo skips, lateral tempo skips, and finally 4-6 hard 10-yard sprints.
6:35pm:	Start throwing. I'd get my catcher and we'd slowly move out to about 180 feet or so, longer if I wanted to. Once I reached max distance, I increased my velocity slowly until I was throwing about 90% effort at 180 feet. I'd start to walk in about 5-10 feet at a time, throwing has hard as I could possibly throw to my catcher.
6:45pm:	Once about 60 feet from my catcher, I'd throw 3-4 fastballs with intent to hurt him. Then, I'd back it down to about 75% and warm up all of my offspeed pitches. After about 5-10 of each, we'd head to the bullpen.

6:50pm: Bullpen would begin. This was scripted exactly as laid out in chapter 13.

6:58pm: Bullpen complete, I'd walk up to the dugout wearing the angriest face I could muster.

7:03pm: Anthem time: Let's go!

CHAPTER 13
HOW TO PRACTICE

There is a very specific method followed by all professional pitchers. They don't just play catch; they always throw to boost weaknesses, hone mechanics, improve arm health and stamina, and maintain optimal sharpness. They do this by mixing pitch intensities and sequences in practice.

More so than mechanics drills, focused practice provides the greatest benefit to a pitcher. It is important to remember that the vast majority of a pitcher's throws will be made in practice – playing catch and throwing bullpens. Most amateur pitchers only focus on good habits while on the bullpen or game mound, but this leaves a lot of wasted practice time.

Consider the following rudimentary math:

Say that a pitcher, on average, throws five days per week and rests two. His career starts at age 8 and lasts until age 18 – 11 full years of baseball. Let's suppose the pitcher takes 12 weeks off from baseball per year, leaving him on the above schedule of five days per week for 40 weeks per year.

Two days per week, only catch is played – an average of 70 total throws each day. The other three days are comprised of two bullpen days and one game day. On each of these three days, 25 warm up throws are made, along with an average of 40 pitches on the mound. This adds up to 335 total throws per week.

So, adding up the above numbers, we get 215 "catch" throws – low-speed throws made while playing catch or warming up. Game and bullpen days add up to 120 throws. So 215 out of 335 total throws is 65%. Thus, the pitcher spends 65% of his life throwing at low-speed, and only 35% throwing at high-speed on the mound. Obviously, this scheme would vary from person to person, and other activities such as long-toss and flat-ground work wouldn't necessarily be deemed "catch." Nonetheless, the point is that the pitcher is going to be defined on his greatest workload, which is, overwhelmingly, low-speed throwing.

If 65% doesn't seem like that big a number, let's consider how those 215 throws add up over the course of a pitcher's career. Eleven years with 40 weeks of throwing at 215 low-speed throws per week adds up to almost 95,000 throws. Another 120 high-speed throws add up to 53,000 throws, leaving us with a difference of 42,000 throws – no insignificant number. What will separate the elite-level pitchers from the rest is what they make of those 95,000 low-speed throws. If these throws are made practicing excellent mechanics, working on developing feel for offspeed pitches, and generally focusing on being a better pitcher, anything is possible.

Coding a Throwing Program

A coding system makes writing throwing programs more concise.

First, we abbreviate as follows:
- Fastball = FB
- Changeup = CH
- Breaking ball (Slider or Curve) = BR

Then, we indicate pitch sequences by grouping pitches into sets. Examples:
- 1 set: 1FB-2BR = 1 fastball followed by 2 breaking balls (3 total pitches)
- 3 sets: 1FB-1CH = Alternate fastball and changeup (6 total pitches)

Lastly, we can indicate location:
- FB/IN = Fastball inside
- CH/OUT = Changeup outside
- BR/DWN = Breaking ball down
- FB/UP = Fastball up
- BR/MID = Breaking ball middle

Optimizing Practice Time: Playing Catch

Rule #1: Always throw exclusively with proper mechanics.

Every lazy throw reinforces poor mechanics and thus does not make the pitcher better. Every throw should be made from the stretch utilizing some form of the pitcher's game mechanics or a drill that reinforces a good habit.

Rule #2: Don't overthrow.

Many pitchers make the mistake of trying to prove their arm strength every single day. Throwing at slower speeds allows more throws to be made before fatigue, giving the pitcher more practice. More quality throws equals more skill. There is nothing wrong with making 100-plus throws during catch as long as the throws are light in effort.

Rule #3: Give targets.

This seems obvious, but many partners will simply stare into the clouds and neglect to give a good target for their throwing partner. Working on the target alignment system in practice is crucial, and it all starts with a solid connection to the focal point.

Rule #4: 90% hit rate.

A pitcher who can't hit his partner's glove during catch will have no chance of hitting his spots in a game. The best pitchers always focus and challenge themselves to never miss – 90% of throws should hit the partner's target during catch.

A Sensible Game of Catch

Throws 1-7:	All FB. Use a mechanics drill that improves upon a bad habit.
Throws 8-15:	All FB. Work from the slide step.
Throws 16-20:	All FB. Work from the windup, leg kick or slide step.
Throws 21-40:	All FB. Stretch out to whatever distance is desired.
Throws 41-70:	Return to distance suitable for pitch work, typically 45-60ft.
(or beyond)	- Work from windup, leg kick or slide step.
	- Ask partner for a target and throw all pitches.
	- Work on engaging the focal point.
	- Use a combination of 1FB-2BR & 1FB-2CH sets.

Optimizing Practice Time: Flat Ground

A "flat-ground" is a bullpen thrown on flat ground at low speed, often at a shorter than regulation distance. Most college and pro pitchers will throw flat-grounds at a 50 foot distance, 10 feet shorter than regulation.

Rule #1: Get down.

Crouch for your partner and have him crouch for you. The flat-ground is a time to work on downhill angle on pitches, which will more closely simulate the release angle seen in games.

Rule #2: Work on weaknesses.

Move the ball in and out, up and down, but focus most specifically on improving weaknesses. Elite pitchers use their flat ground and bullpen sessions to find solutions to problems seen in recent outings.

Rule #3: Keep it short.

Flat-grounds fulfill a specific purpose – more game-like than catch, but less intense than a bullpen. Some pitchers throw a short (10-15 pitch) flat-ground every single day. Others like them slightly longer (20-25 pitches) the day before an outing or to replace a bullpen with less effort. Regardless, keep it short and focused – 25 throws maximum.

Rule #4: Low-effort.

Relievers throw more flat-ground sessions than starters because they have to make sure they are fresh on any given day. Starters can plan out the four days between starts, but relievers cannot. So, relievers throw more low-effort flat grounds than bullpens, and both starters and relievers keep the intensity very low – typically 50%.

A Sensible Flat-Ground Workout

Warm-up throws 1-7: All FB. Use a mechanics drill that improves upon a bad habit.

Warm-up throws 8-15: All FB. Work from the slide step.

Warm-up throws 16-20: All FB. Work from the windup, leg kick or slide step.

Flat-ground session: Return to distance suitable for pitch work, typically 45-60ft.

(*20 throws*)
- Work from windup, leg kick or slide step – whichever is most troublesome.
- Work on engaging the focal point.
- Work in and out, up and down, but spend the most time on weaknesses.
- Use a combination of 1FB-2BR & 1FB-2CH sets, or call pitches like in a game.

Optimizing Practice Time: Bullpens

Bullpens are practice sessions thrown off the mound. Bullpens are high intensity, typically about 70% effort but ranging from 50%-100%.

Rule #1: Long pens are for preseason only.

For starting pitchers, preseason is only one time of year when it's appropriate to throw a bullpen of more than 40 pitches. Starters must get their conditioning up by increasing their pitch count before opening day, so bullpens during the preseason may reach as many as 80 pitches. All other times of year, bullpens must be much shorter.

Rule #2: All in-season bullpens are 35 pitches or less.

A common mistake made by amateurs is throwing long bullpens. During a competitive season, there is no reason to ever go beyond 35 pitches, and even 35 pitches is a bit much. The magic number is 25-30 – get on the mound, quickly address weakness, then get back off. Throwing arms have limited energy and need to heal between outings – stress levels must stay low between in-game performances. Throwing too much between outings will add fatigue and stress to the arm.

Rule #3: Low-effort; Be a cheetah.

During the season, the pitcher should be careful to complete each bullpen with the least energy expenditure possible to do the job. This refers to energy (glycogen) stored within the key muscles of the arm and shoulder. Sometimes, a pitch needs to be thrown at full-speed to work the kinks out. But, most of the time a bullpen thrown at 50-70% will do the job of perfecting a pitcher's feel and preparing him for his next outing. Professional pitchers almost never throw above 70% on the mound between starts. Cheetah mentality is key – conserve energy and only throw hard when absolutely necessary during the season.

Rule #4: Get better.

Too often, pitchers use their bullpen sessions simply to re-inflate the ego. Bullpens must be short, and as such quickly working on weaknesses must be the primary objective. The most attention should be paid to the weakest pitches and locations in the arsenal while not neglecting the strongest pitches and locations. Having a set bullpen workout, as outlined below, is helpful. But, the bullpen should always be tailored to the skillset of the pitcher and his strengths and weaknesses.

A Sensible Bullpen Workout

Flat warm-up throws 1-5:	All FB. Use a mechanics drill that improves upon a bad habit.
Flat warm-up throws 6-25:	All FB. Work from the windup, leg kick or slide step.
	- Move back in distance until arm is warmed up to initial bullpen intensity.
Flat warm-up throws 26-37:	12 throws: 4 sets: 1FB-1CH-1BR
Bullpen session:	3 Pitches: 3 FB down the middle.
(*30 pitches*)	6 Pitches: 3 sets: 1FB/IN-1FB/OUT
	6 Pitches: 3 sets: 1FB/IN-2CH
	6 Pitches: 3 sets: 1FB/OUT-2BR (substitute CH if no BR)
	9 Pitches: Work on weaknesses/pitch sequences/simulated game.

Optimizing Practice Time: Pregame for Starters

Want an easy way to spot a rookie? He's the guy throwing 100 pitches in his pregame bullpen; it never fails. Pregame is a crucial time where optimum volume and intensity can make or break a pitcher. Inexperienced pitchers will tire themselves out before even getting into the game – they throw too early, too much and too hard.

Rule #1: A warm-up shortens the warm-up.

It's important to use a full-body warm up routine – the warmer the body is when it's time to start throwing, the fewer throws it will take to get loose. Remember that fewer warm up throws will preserve more energy for the game. And, muscle contraction speed increases with muscle temperature – the warmer your muscles are, the higher velocity potential you will possess.

Rule #2: Adrenaline is an old friend.

Adrenaline is great – pregame excitement aids the warm up process and reduces the amount of throws needed. The more nervous the pitcher, the more he can count on his body responding with hormones to warm him up quickly.

Rule #3: Back it up.

Every pitcher is different. While extreme long-toss is not required, getting stretched out by throwing longer distances is a good idea. Long toss is typically more helpful in the warm-up process than simply throwing harder at shorter distances. Throwing at longer distances helps build arm extension, which is crucial to throwing at maximum velocity.

Rule #4: Light it up.

The pitcher must throw at 100% velocity on the mound before worrying about location and offspeed pitches. I take this stance because in my experience with throwing velocity, a pitcher's velocity does not reach a true 100% level until 10-plus throws at maximal effort. Thus, I feel that

the first 4-6 fastballs of the pregame bullpen should be thrown as hard as possible with no regard to location. Then, when the arm is moving at maximal or near-maximal levels, the pitcher can dial in his control. The pregame bullpen should prepare the starter to locate all pitches at full-speed; a 75-90% effort bullpen will not accomplish this.

Rule #5: Mix it up.

Mix all the pitches in the pregame bullpen, and spend extra time on those pitches that are a struggle to throw with typical break or location. Not every pitch will be at its best, so spend extra pitches attempting to boost the weak links.

A Sensible Pregame Warm-Up

Flat warm-up throws #1-5:   All FB. Use a mechanics drill that improves upon a bad habit.

Flat warm-up throws #6-25: All FB. Work from the windup, leg kick or slide step.
                            - Move back in distance until arm is warm to initial bullpen intensity.

Flat warm-up throws #26-37: 12 throws: 4 sets: 1FB-1CH-1BR
                            - Approximately 50-75% effort

Bullpen session: 4-6 pitches: Wind up. All FB thrown as hard as possible.
(*30-40 pitches*)   3 Pitches: Wind-up. 1 set: 1FB/IN-1CH/MID-1CH/DN
                            3 Pitches: Wind-up: 1 set: 1FB/OUT-1BR/MID-1BR/DN
                            3 Pitches: Slide step: 1 set: 1FB/OUT-1CH/MID-1CH/DN
                            3 Pitches: Slide step: 1 set: 1FB/IN-1BR/MID-1BR/DN
                            3-4 Pitches: Slide step: Throw more of whichever offspeed pitch is weaker.
                            10-15 Pitches: Wind-up: Work on weaknesses/pitch sequences/simulated game at 100% intensity.

Optimizing Practice Time: Pregame – Relievers

"Pregame" for a reliever is actually during the game, but a reliever's pregame is the brief few moments before being inserted into the action.

Rule #1: Conserve warmth.

Relievers should wear a jacket unless the hot sun makes it too uncomfortable. A warmer body means shorter warm-up time, and the bullpen is a poor venue to run around and perform a rigorous warm-up. Most amateur ballparks won't even have a dedicated bullpen area.

Rule #2: Short and intense.

Any type of whole-body warm-up before being inserted into the game must be short and intense; the goal is to get as much blood moving as fast as possible.

Relievers also must be prepared to enter the game in a hurry – within the time it takes for one or two hitters to complete their at-bats. This means that throwing warm-ups must also be short and intense.

Rule #3: Save it for the game.

The relief pitcher is given eight warm up pitches on the game mound, so getting 100% ready in the bullpen isn't necessary. Pro pitchers often get about 90% ready in the bullpen then finish their warm-up on the game mound so that they don't expend extra energy.

A Sensible Pregame Warm-Up

Rapid-fire catch: Throws #1-5: All FB. From the slide step throwing back and forth quickly at low-intensity.

Flat warm-up throws #6-15: Mix of all pitches; Slide step or leg kick
- Increase velocity/intensity until about 75% effort.

Mound warm-up pitches #16-25: Increase velocity/intensity until about 90%.
4 Pitches: 1 Set: 4FB
3 Pitches: 1 Set: 3CH
3 Pitches: 1 Set: 3BR
- Additional pitches as needed to get ready.

Note: Alternating pitches, while ideal in practice sessions, is not as efficient on time or energy for relievers. Inserting a fastball between every offspeed pitch would add a lot of additional pitches to the warm-up, which relievers need to avoid.

Optimizing Practice Time: In-Game Warm-Ups for All Pitchers

In-game warm-ups aren't just to get the arm back up to full-speed after a long sit on the bench. A good warm-up strategy will help the pitcher address weaknesses and improve his arsenal as the game progresses.

Rule #1: Heat up fast.

Pitchers only get six pitches between innings; they shouldn't make any pitches at less than 90% effort. The first pitch, when the pitcher is at his coldest, can be of lesser intensity than the subsequent lot. However, each warm-up pitch should have a purpose, and low-intensity throws don't help the pitcher warm up fast enough.

Rule #2: Don't have to throw them all.

Six pitches is not a lot. As such, it's best to work on the offspeed pitch that needs the most work and trust that the other offerings are still in good shape from the previous inning.

Rule #3: Finish from the wind-up.

Conventional wisdom is to throw the "coming down" pitch (thrown to second base by the catcher) from the stretch. But, because this is the last warm-up a pitcher will get, and because his first real pitch will be from the wind up, we should make this last warm-up from the wind up as well.

Rule #4: Work on missed locations.

Can't hit the outside corner with the fastball? Can throw the curveball down in the zone but not for a strike? Spend the warm-up working exclusively on these trouble locations.

<u>A Sensible Between-Innings Warm-Up</u>

If both offspeed pitches need equal work:
>Pitch 1 – Wind-up: Fastball 90% effort
>Pitch 2 – Wind-up: Fastball 100% effort
>Pitch 3 – Slide step: Changeup 100% effort
>Pitch 4 – Slide step: Breaking Ball 100% effort
>Pitch 5 – Slide step: Breaking Ball 100% effort
>Pitch 6 – Wind-up: Changeup 100% effort

If one pitch needs more work than the other (change up needs work in example below):
>Pitch 1 – Wind-up: Fastball 90% effort
>Pitch 2 – Wind-up: Fastball 100% effort
>Pitch 3 – Slide step: Changeup 100% effort
>Pitch 4 – Slide step: Changeup 100% effort
>Pitch 5 – Slide step: Fastball 100% effort
>Pitch 6 – Wind-up: Changeup 100% effort

<u>Optimizing Practice Time – Long Toss</u>

Long toss has become a topic for heated debate in recent years – some love it, some hate it. A poll of Major League players would likely reveal that many use it religiously. I believe long toss has tremendous value. Yet, before we get into my argument for the efficacy of long toss, let's first discuss: *what is long toss?*

Long Toss, Loosely Defined

Long toss can be most basically defined as throwing long distances on a higher than normal trajectory. This vague definition could potentially mean lots of things, but I think most of us agree that "long toss" implies just that – throwing relatively long distances. I'm going to define this as distances that represent 75% or more of a pitcher's maximum distance throw. Many Major League teams define long toss as throwing at a 120-foot distance. But, considering the vast arm strength of these pitchers, 120 feet is, in reality, short. If a pitcher overthrows first base the ball will fly farther than 120 feet. Rather, a better definition is: throwing at 75% or greater of one's maximum throwing distance. That's what I would call long toss.

Theory of Long Toss

Long toss, in theory, provides the user with a few different training benefits:
- Increased extension (reaching out to a distant target)
- Resembles shoulder tilt seen while throwing downhill on mound
- Encourages fluidity of arm action
- Encourages slow and gradual warm up
- Provides a velocity goal (throw farther to throw harder)
- Hitting a partner at long distances demands greater accuracy
- It is governed by autoregulation (more in this in a bit)
- Teaches the pitcher to keep weight back longer

How to Long Toss – The Jaeger Method

The biggest proponent of long toss in the baseball industry is Alan Jaeger. Alan has taken what was a loosely defined methodology and shaped it into a specific training protocol. As such, I feel strongly that the best way to perform long toss is by using Jaeger's method. It is recommended that you visit his website at http://www.jaegersports.com/Arm-Strength-and-Conditioning/ for more in-depth instruction. I have personally used this method for many years and have been a lifetime long-tosser. I only endorse methods that are proven, through experience or otherwise, to be effective. The following is my interpretation of the Jaeger method.

The Stretching Out Phase

1. Start very close to your throwing partner and gently begin to toss.
2. The arm will start to gradually overthrow your partner as it gets warm and loose. This is the signal to start moving back.
3. Move back gradually at the pace dictated by how your arm feels.
4. Arc the ball at a high release angle (30-40°) while your partner continues to slowly move back. The point at this phase is to reach, extend, and be relaxed - not throw bullets.
5. Do not rush the process. Take as much time as is needed to reach maximum distance.
6. At maximum distance, spend as much time as you'd like throwing at a high arc, reaching out to challenge yourself.

The Pull Down Phase

1. Once at maximum distance and ready to come back in, the goal is to compress the max-distance throw into a shorter, bullet-throw.
2. Lower the focal point on your partner and drive the ball at a downward angle.
3. Do not slow the arm down – throw as hard as possible while maintaining the fluidity, extension and arm speed from the high-arc, max-distance throws.
4. Come in gradually, a few feet and a few throws at a time. Take as long as is needed.
5. It will be very difficult to hit your partner while keeping arm speed at 100%. It will be necessary to drastically lower the focal point as distances close in on 150 feet or less. This may mean aiming to throw into the grass up to 30 feet in front of your partner.
6. Continue to throw hard, challenging yourself to keep the max-effort arm extension and speed as you get close to your partner.
7. It is recommended that you don't get closer than 70 feet to your partner if you're a very hard thrower. It can be dangerous for those not used to catching high speeds.

Reasons Long Toss Can Benefit a Pitcher

Here are a few reasons why I believe long toss can benefit a pitcher:

1. Teaches Autoregulation

Autoregulation is a crucial term that is most seen in strength training. It refers to one adjusting his training workload according to how he feels that day. Strength training provides simple examples:

On Monday, I felt strong. In a maximum-effort set, I squatted 400 pounds.

On Thursday, I squatted again. But, 375 pounds felt as heavy as 400 did, so I did not push beyond 375 and called that my "max" for the day.

Too often, people get caught up trying to meet or exceed their lifetime maximums every session and get hurt because they don't listen when their body is telling them that it's fatigued or overworked. You can't be at your absolute best every single day!

Because long toss requires a gradual, relaxed warm up and has no set number of throws, it can be easily autoregulated. If one day, the arm feels great and can throw 350 feet, awesome! If the next time out 300 feet feels like a chore, then don't go beyond that. All that matters is stretching out, reaching that day's max, and learning to listen to how the body feels. This is a good lesson for pitchers – just because you hit 95mph last time, doesn't mean your body is capable of it today. Every day the body has a different limit that must not be exceeded.

2. Builds Extension

From my work teaching amateur pitchers to throw harder, I've found that extension toward the target is a crucial determinant of velocity. This means reaching forward to the target rather than attempting to yank the ball downward. The best teacher I've found for this, besides using a radar gun in an indoor setting, is long toss. Long toss, with the target way in the distance, cues the thrower to automatically reach out and not be lazy with the finish of his throw. It is much easier to reach maximum speeds attempting to hit a distant target then to throw to a short target. When the target is close, the perceived amount of effort to hit the target is small. When the target is far in the distance, the perception is that a greater amount of effort is required. I have found that it is easier to achieve higher velocities after long tossing than simply warming up at a short distance.

3. Teaches Fluidity

All high-velocity movements have a unique combination of fluid motion and intense muscle contraction. You cannot effectively sprint while tense, throw while tense, swing while tense, or jump while tense. Many pitchers, when they try to throw harder, end up throwing with less velocity because they tense their muscles, resulting in an arm that does not move efficiently. The hardest throwers have a perfect balance of intense, powerful muscle contraction with optimal relaxation.

Sure, one could tense up during long toss. But, starting very softly, moving back gradually and practicing the long, high-arc lobbed throws teaches the pitcher to stay calm while throwing with minimal effort. Lobbed throws are, by nature, relaxed. This transfers into pitchers who learn to stay relaxed and fluid while throwing at long distances and high efforts.

4. Teaches Release Adjustment

When moving from the max-distance throw to the pull down phase, it takes quite a lot of effort to compress throws from 40 feet off the ground to only 4-6 feet. Attempting to crunch the ball lower and lower while maintaining arm speed is good practice for driving the ball down in the strike zone.

Additionally, learning to use the focal point to one's advantage is central to the pull down phase of long toss. Pitchers need to adjust their focal point on breaking balls, change ups, and poorly-located fastballs during the game. While long tossing, if one doesn't move the focal point drastically lower during pull-down throws, the ball will sail over the partner. Learning to not overthrow the partner has great carry over to effective use of focal points during games.

5. Increases Accuracy

One of my mentors talked with me about how in the Vietnam War, one of his platoon members, standing a few feet from him, was hit in the chest with a rocket fired from a mile away. "Over such a long distance, the difference between which one of us lived and died was an insignificant millimeter in that soldier's aim."

When throwing a long distance, release point inconsistencies of only an inch can result in a ball that pulls many feet off target. For two pitchers to long toss and consistently hit each other without moving is an impressive feat of accuracy. Mechanics have to be very sound and repeatable to effectively long toss without chasing errant throws all day.

6. Provides a Unique Stimulus

Training the same way for a lifetime may satisfy the rule of specificity of training, but it does not supply the body with an adequate stimulus to keep progressing. It is my opinion that throwing at different angles helps keep the arm refreshed and stimulated in ways that help build more velocity. This is based on my observations of this phenomenon in strength training and other areas of practice – exercise variation and periodization allows for plateaus to be breached. I am confident that future research will corroborate changes in muscle activation patterns in long toss versus flat ground versus mound throwing. These changes in activation could have a positive effect on the development of throwing velocity.

Rebutting the Detractors of Long Toss

There are Major League organizations that refuse to allow their pitchers to long toss. There are also many pitching experts and coaches who believe it to be ineffective, inappropriate and possibly dangerous. These claims and my counterclaims can be summed as follows:

1. "Long Toss is Inappropriate"

The crux of this matter is the principle of specificity, which states that the best way to increase skill is to perform exercise that most closely mirrors it. In pitching, the most specific exercise is pitching from a mound at 60 feet, 6 inches. Long toss detractors say that by throwing at an uphill angle on flat ground, the movement is inappropriate practice for downhill throwing off of a mound.

This argument, however, is open to attack on a few fronts. Other training principles, such as the principle of diminishing returns states that when an athlete becomes very well conditioned at a given exercise, his gains will taper off as he reaches his genetic potential. Throwing off a mound as the only form of throwing practice, therefore, could be subject to diminishing returns. As we all know, if more throwing caused more velocity, professional pitchers would throw harder as their careers wore on. We know this is not the case for several reasons, including wear and tear on muscles, tendons and ligaments, but also possibly because the arm is no longer stimulated in a new way. Most pitchers do throw harder from throwing more often, but only as they reach physical maturity. Most pitchers plateau at velocity levels by age 21 or so, if not before.

The principle of variation states that for new performance gains to continue, the exercise regimen must be varied with new exercises and activities to stimulate the body. While specific training is, of course, good training, variation must be present in a training program for the body to continue to progress. Long-toss detractors do allow their pitchers to throw on flat-ground between outings, which arguably comprises more throws during a long career than their mound throws. This is inconsistent with their fervor that only specific throwing (off a mound) is appropriate practice.

2. "Long Toss is Ineffective"

Detractors of long toss discuss that because long toss is less specific to throwing downhill on a mound, that any increased throwing distance will not transfer to the mound. This line of reasoning is flawed because a major part of throwing a baseball at high speed is about the intent to apply high force. Any throwing exercise or drill that teaches a pitcher to apply more of his available force to the baseball will have a positive effect on his throwing velocity at any angle – uphill, downhill or flat. The act of attempting to throw a ball farther is a good drill to teach more force application – more distance means the pitcher was successful in applying greater force. If he can then summon this same technique with his downhill mechanics (he will have to practice on a mound), then long toss will have had a positive effect.

Additionally, think of the accuracy required to hit your partner in the chest from 300 feet away. The release point window for the ball to fly almost perfectly on target over such a distance is remarkable. Just a few inches or degrees off line, at that distance, can result in accuracy errors of multiple feet. If one can be accurate from longer distances, shouldn't it make throwing accurately at shorter distances easier? It is reasonable to conclude that long toss can help improve accuracy.

3. "Long Toss is Dangerous"

A recent study by the ASMI showed increased stress at the elbow during higher angle throws. The study by Fleisig, et al, 2011, can be found here:

Biomechanical comparison of baseball pitching and long-toss: implications for training and rehabilitation. Journal of Orthopedic Sports Physical Therapy. 2011 May;41(5):296-303. doi: 10.2519/jospt.2011.3568. Epub 2011 Jan 5.

Although this study concludes that long toss results in higher elbow stress, there is yet no causal link between pitching injuries and long toss. Greater stress does not necessarily mean injurious. Every pitcher has a different capacity for stress that must not be exceeded, and it is unknown if the extra stress exceeds this limit, especially when compared to the rigors of throwing competitively for 1000+ pitches during a summer.
More research needs to be done on this topic. Anecdotally, thousands of pitchers claim that their arms feel and perform better when long toss is part of their routine. Conversely, there are also pitchers that don't like or find benefit in it. There are many sporting activities and training exercises that increase stress on the joints to elicit a training effect. It is unknown, yet possible that exercises and drills that cause increased arm stress can still be part of an effective and safe training program. It is my recommendation that every player merge research with experience to find what works best for him.

Integrating Long Toss into the Throwing Routine

Hopefully you're convinced that long toss is worth addition to your practice plan. You'll need to place it sensibly into your weekly regimen. Here are a few guidelines on integration:

1. Above All: Autoregulate

Some players long toss the day after a start. Some players long toss once per week, some twice, some three times. It all depends on the player, their pitching workload, and their ability to recover. Better-conditioned, stronger pitchers can throw more between outings without adverse effects or undue fatigue. This is where strength training, conditioning and throwing meet to enhance one another.

Add one day of long toss at first and see how it affects your arm during games and during the week. No one can predict how it will affect each individual. If all is great, add in more long toss days at your discretion. Being overzealous and jumping into three days of long toss, two game days and two bullpens is not the way to approach it.

2. For Starters - Allow a Buffer of One Day

At first it's best to not long toss until the second day after a start, or the second day before a start. Allow one rest day before or after starting. If, during the season, one can handle long tossing twice between starts, so be it. But, make sure to work up to that volume and balance bullpens, games, catch and long toss accordingly. This is going to be largely up to you and your arm to determine the optimal dose.

Most 5-Day rotation starters do this: Day 0: Start
Day 1: Off or light catch
Day 2: Long toss
Day 3: Bullpen
Day 4: Flat ground or light catch
Day 5: Start

Most 7-Day rotation starters do this: Day 0: Start
Day 1: Off or light catch
Day 2: Heavy long toss
Day 3: Long bullpen
Day 4: Moderate or light long toss
Day 5: Short bullpen
Day 6: Off or light catch or flat ground
Day 7: Start

3. For Relievers – Buffer with Rest, When Possible

If in relief, it is harder to plan one's weekly workload. But, attempt to long toss only when you have one full day between the next possible outing. If this is not possible, shorter, less intense sessions of long toss are a good idea. These less-intense days can involve sub-maximal distances and a short or no pull-down phase. Save the all-out days of long toss for when you know you have at least one day of rest until the next possible outing.

Most relievers do this:	Day 1: Pitch | Light catch or flat ground
(*throwing done during pre-game*)	Day 2: Off | Light long toss
	Day 3: Pitch | Flat ground
	Day 4: Off | Light long toss or flat ground
	Day 5: Pitch | Light catch
	Day 6: Off | Heavy long Toss
	Day 7: Off | Flat ground

4. During the Off-Season

If you aren't pitching in the off-season (you should not be!), long toss can be done up to three or four days per week. But, again – listen to your arm. If you aren't capable of it, then don't do it. Start with more days of light catch or flat ground throwing and less days of long toss, then skew to more long toss and less catch and flat ground as your arm becomes used to the higher workload. Saying, "I want to increase my velocity through long-toss" is not an excuse to be stupid and push your body beyond it's limits. Like everything, gradually increase the acceptable dose until optimal dosing is reached.

CHAPTER 14

STRENGTH TRAINING & CONDITIONING

Strength training plays a key role in developing strength, body control and overall athleticism. Getting stronger increases the pitcher's ability to produce force and control his body; this will transfer into pitching velocity and mechanical consistency. Even very simple strength training programs can yield excellent gains if performed at high intensity and with proper, safe technique.

Why Strength Training and Lean Body Mass is Essential

Athletic prowess is highly associated with a simple algorithm: $F = M \times A$: force = mass times acceleration. Athletes who produce higher levels of force in shorter amounts of time run faster, change direction quicker, hit harder, swing faster, and throw at higher velocities. While coordination, dexterity and intelligence are all crucial in sport-specific skill, force production is a central physical attribute. The throwing arm is an extension of the body, and all muscles work together to create as much force as quickly as possible, resulting in a pulse of explosive energy.

"Sport-Specific" is Misunderstood

Sport-specific training is a bit of a misnomer, as the goal of strength training is not to mimic sporting activities and add resistance to them. The easiest way to ruin a baseball or golf swing or change pitching mechanics in an adverse way is by adding resistance to the motion. Throwing a baseball is a highly powerful but fluid motion, one that can easily be disrupted if we force the limbs to move against bands, weights or other forms of resistance. If we add unnatural resistance during training to a fluid sporting motion, the motion can change and result in a reduction in efficiency.

The goal of strength training is to increase athleticism, size, strength and force output. We accomplish these goals by performing strength training movements that both strengthen muscles and general movement patterns. We then make stronger muscles and quality movements "sport-specific" by going out and separately playing the sport. The body will learn to integrate the new muscle and strength as efficiently as possible within the fluid mechanics of the sports movement.

Another consideration is the overall picture of what the athlete experiences in both his sport and in the weight room. Sprinters, for example, sprint in practice and in competition – it's the most "specific" training method available to them. Yet, most would agree that only performing the sporting action, sprinting in this case, leaves an athlete underdeveloped as new stimuli are needed to keep muscles from stagnating.

Sprinters need to do things other than just sprint or their bodies will adapt and plateau to the bodyweight sprinting stimulus. A good addition to sprinters' training would be to lift weights to add strength and force output in the legs, which they can then, in turn, apply on the track. They get sprinting in practice and heavy lifting in training, a formula proven to work by the world's best sprint coaches.

Pitchers are the same way. Too many coaches and parents choose to only use explosive training methods in the weight room – plyometrics, endless medicine ball throws, etc. Though these elements are important and have their place, they mimic what the pitcher already gets every day in his sport – highly explosive movements with low-resistance (a baseball is only 5oz). If a pitcher is making 100 explosive, high-speed rotational movements every day at practice and in his games, why continue to train that same way in the weight room? Rather, it is good training to provide what he isn't getting – heavier strength training to increase strength and force output, much like the sprinter. In summary, when we make training too much like the sport, we lose the training effect altogether because the body needs new stimuli to continue to increase force output.

But, bigger isn't always better.

It's important to note a few things about pitchers – while size matters, bigger muscles don't always mean more velocity, and many of the world's best athletes are not the strongest in the weight room. But, for those with unrealized potential and for most amateur athletes who haven't "filled out," they will gain a significant amount of throwing velocity from increasing lean body mass. There's a reason 12 year-olds with great mechanics cannot throw at the same velocity as 18 year-olds with great mechanics – they lack the muscular force to produce high speeds and the joint stability to control it.

For most amateurs, an increase in muscle mass will correlate to an increase in velocity. Although there are outliers seen in all levels of baseball, such as Tim Lincecum, who throws exceptionally hard with a small frame, taller and heavier pitchers generally throw harder. It is therefore a prudent goal to carry as much muscle mass as one can without sacrificing flexibility – it almost always helps, and rarely hurts if done properly.

Your author went from a weight of 170 pounds as a high school senior to 205 pounds as a 27-year old. The 170-pound version was capable of speeds of 78-83 mph; the 205-pound version is capable of speeds peaking in the mid-90s. This same anecdote can be found across countless collegiate, high school and middle school pitchers – when they gain weight and get stronger, velocity increases. While causation is difficult to infer, there is a strong case for being bigger and stronger and it makes little sense to choose to be small and weak.

However, there comes a tipping point where greater muscle mass does not lead to greater throwing velocity. The goal is to increase lean body mass and strength to increase force production. Once an athlete is big and strong for his size (this is unique to each individual), his gains will begin to taper off. The hard-throwing pitcher has an ideal combination of muscular size, strength, explosiveness and athleticism. The way in which the size and strength is built is also very important.

What Do Scouts Want to See?

Projectable

"Will throw harder as he fills out."
"Very projectable frame."
"Needs to get stronger."
"May not be durable."

These are all common notes that would be seen on the scouting card of a high school pitcher. Scouts draft "prospects" – players they believe have a high potential ceiling due to their raw physical abilities. Players who are tall but thin, with long arms and legs, are very likely, very projectable, to throw harder as they "fill out." This means that as they add some muscle mass to their lanky body, more velocity will be realized. This is very often the case, which is why MLB organizations have no problem giving millions of dollars to high school pitchers who throw 90 miles per hour with immature bodies. Many of these pitchers can be found reaching into the mid-90s one to two years later once they add muscle mass from strength training and physical maturity.

Many players with lots of raw ability turn themselves into draft-picks or college prospects once they learn to utilize the weight room. And, because amateur players are almost always still growing, putting on weight is easy; their high hormone levels somewhat mimic the effect of steroids. Players in my academy routinely put on 15 pounds every offseason of their high school career, partly due to natural growth and partly due to quality, consistent strength training and nutritional counseling.

Durability

The other factor scouts consider is durability – how likely a player is to endure a season without suffering an injury or a decrease in performance. Many players find it difficult to pitch for 140 games every summer, in the heat with few days off, without getting arm deadness, chronic pain or a major injury. The money MLB teams invest in a player is wasted if he cannot take the field due to injury. So, they look to pick players whose bodies are more likely to hold up to many years of competitive stress. Bigger, stronger, denser bodies are more likely to withstand such difficult conditions.

Boxing is a somewhat apt analogy – which player is more likely to last ten rounds with a great boxer like Mike Tyson – a 147lb Welterweight or a 210lb Heavyweight? Even if skill is equal among the challengers, obviously the heavier fighter can take more punishment before succumbing to Tyson's blows. The theory behind larger pitchers being more durable is basically that having more muscle mass and better leverage to perform the same job spares the passive structures. More muscle mass and longer limbs take stress off the bones, tendons and ligaments, which are the first to break down.

How to Build Size and Strength

Bodybuilders train to build muscular size, and they have it down to a reproducible science. However, because bodybuilders optimize muscle growth by utilizing higher repetitions performed at a slow pace, their methodology is not ideal for athletes. Athletes need to learn to move heavy loads quickly, and light loads even faster. This teaches their bodies to apply more force with greater speed. For this reason, athletes should focus their strength training around multi-jointed movements in a low-to-moderate repetition range that allows higher resistance. Sets with fewer repetitions also allow the athlete to work at higher intensity before succumbing to fatigue. Heavy loads and high speeds, which build strength, size and explosiveness, cannot be maintained at higher repetition ranges (greater than six in most cases). With this in mind, recommendations for athletes are as follows:

Repetition Ranges

1-5 Repetitions: Absolute strength is built in this range (best for advanced lifters).
4-8 Repetitions: Strength and muscular size is built in this range.
8-10 Repetitions: Muscular size, and some strength, is built in this range (best for novices).

I see the biggest gains for athletes of all ability levels in the range of 4-8 repetitions. These allow for heavy weights and a higher volume of overall work. Rule of thumb is that the number of sets will increase as repetitions decrease. For sake of simplicity, break a workout into one of the four following set and rep schemes. Again – we don't have to delve deeply into muscle physiology and training theory to steer in the right direction.

It's also crucial to understand that when one prescribes X reps, the resistance used should be enough to allow one to perform X+1 or 2 reps without form breaking down. So, in a set of 3 repetitions, weight should be heavy enough where the user could perform 4 or 5 perfect repetitions, but not more.

Ideal Sets and Repetition Schemes

5x3 – Five sets of three reps.
4x6 – Four sets of six reps.
3x8 – Three sets of eight reps.
3x10 – Three sets of ten reps.

If an athlete needs more size, he should stay in the higher end – six reps and above. If he needs more maximal strength but is already big, then sets of six reps and below would be ideal. If he trains multiple times per week, it would be advantageous to get some higher and some lower repetition sets. This should be set up by a qualified local strength coach.

Exercise Choices

The best exercises for athletes are multi-jointed varieties that require the body to work as an entire system. Isolating muscles, such as in the biceps curl exercise, is a practice best left to bodybuilders who need size above all else. For athletes, muscle will be built and the body made strong when resistance is loaded across as many muscles as possible. This is what many call "functional training," in which the body increases its ability to function holistically. Terminology aside, athletes will see more of their size and strength transfer over to sport-specific activities (pitching a baseball) when they utilize the "big lifts" in their training. Specifically, these are:

- Squats and variations
- Chin ups, rows and variations
- Weighted carries
- Jumping
- Weighted sled pushes
- Deadlifts and variations
- Push ups and push up variations
- Sprinting
- Throwing objects

Exercise Program Layout

Strength training programming is beyond the scope of this book. But, I will briefly square the circle and provide guidelines for assembling a simple training program. For novice lifters, it is imperative that they train under the guidance of a qualified strength coach. Qualified coaches are somewhat rare, so it is best to do copious investigative work before hiring a coach.

Exercise Categorization

Push: Movement in which the arms push the body away from a fixed point, or a weight away from the body.

Muscles developed: arms, chest, core.
Examples: push ups, bench press, dumbbell bench press

Pictured: Push Up

Pull: Pulling a weight toward the body or the body toward a fixed object or bar.

Muscles developed: back, arms, forearms
Examples: chin up, barbell row, dumbbell row, cable row

Pictured: Barbell Row (left), Chin Up (right)

Quadriceps-Dominant: Movement that chiefly recruits the front of the thighs, such as squatting or lunging.

Muscles developed: quadriceps, glutes, hamstrings, back, core
Examples: back squat, front squat, lunges, backward sled pull

Pictured: Back Squat (left), Front Squat (center, Backward Sled Pull (right)

Core: Movement that specifically targets the midsection. Core strengthening is present in high quantities in all other multi-joint movements.

Muscles developed: abdominals and obliques
Examples: planks, medicine ball throws, roll-outs

Pictured: Medicine Ball Throw

195

<u>Hip-Dominant</u>: Movement that chiefly recruits the backside of the thighs. This is typically a
"hip-hinging" type movement typified by more bend at the hips than knees.

Muscles developed:	glutes, hamstrings, back, core, forearms
Examples:	deadlift, Romanian deadlift, hamstring curl, broad jump, forward sled push

Pictured: Deadlift (left), Romanian Deadlift (right)

<u>Weighted Carry</u>: Carrying or holding heavy or odd-shaped objects
for time or distance.

Muscles developed:	forearms and musculature of the hands, back, core
Examples:	walking with dumbbells, holding a heavy barbell for time, holding any odd-shaped implement that is difficult to grip

Pictured: Dumbbell Hold

The above six movement categories have a tremendous amount of overlap with one another because of their whole-body muscle recruitment. For this reason, they should be the foundation of a strength program. By performing multi-joint exercises of the above categories, all major muscles will be strengthened and developed, and the body will achieve relative balance. Pushing and pulling movements work opposite sides of the body, as do quadriceps and hip-dominant movements. Performing one of each of the above would keep the body balanced.

Understanding how and why strength training can improve performance is critical. Utilizing the most effective set and repetition ranges with the most effective movement patterns for balanced musculature will provide a good starting point.

Sample programs will not be provided in this book because there are too many variables and individual differences that need to be addressed before safe recommendations can be made. But, if you have a coach or are experienced in strength training, make sure that your program falls somewhere within the above guidelines. There are many other movements that are valuable in strength training for pitchers, but again – the fundamental six are listed above, the ones that will provide the most benefit for the most people.

Conditioning

Conditioning is important in all sports. Pitching, and baseball in general, is an anaerobic activity, which simply means that it involves short intervals of very high intensity movement followed by intervals of rest. A pitcher starts his windup and throws as hard as he can, completing the entire motion in about 1.5 seconds. He then receives the ball back from the catcher and completes a between-pitch routine that lasts roughly 15-30 seconds. This is anaerobic exercise – short bouts of high-intensity exercise, repeated over and over with rest.

This is very different from aerobic exercise like bicycling or jogging, in which one sustains a low-level of effort for a long period of time. Conventional wisdom had pitchers running long distances to prepare for a start in which they would spend two hours on the mound pitching. But, in reality, a pitcher only pitches for perhaps 3-4 minutes combined in a 100-pitch outing. The rest of those two hours is rest, retrieving the ball, planning strategy, or fielding the position. It doesn't make sense to train aerobically for such a contest.

Additionally, distance running teaches the body to move slowly. We want the exact opposite – a very explosive body with high force output. Training with distance running will not only train the wrong energy system (aerobic instead of anaerobic), but also decrease the pitcher's explosiveness toward the plate. We don't want either of those outcomes.

Running Guidelines

There are many benefits one can derive from distance running, most notably increased cardiac output, which is the ability of ones heart to pump more blood per stroke. Larger stroke volume means muscles are fed oxygen and nutrients more efficiently – a good thing no matter the goals of the athlete. Yet, it does not increase muscular force output.

Sprinting increases an athlete's explosiveness by requiring him to apply 100% of available force as quickly as possible. Sprinting is a great compliment to strength training in that it applies newly built strength to a fundamental athletic movement. In short, it is one of the best things any athlete of any sport can do to increase high-speed coordination. And, a sprinting regimen will properly condition a pitcher for what he needs to do in a game – move as fast as possible for a short time (then repeat).

But, because aerobic exercise does have numerous health benefits, it's not necessary to be dog-matic and rule it out completely, nor will a distance run here and there ruin a training program.

Basically, it can be summed as such:

Run distance every day, and you'll become less explosive and improperly conditioned for pitching. Your body will become used to moving itself and external objects (weights, bats, balls) slowly.

Run sprints every day, and you'll become more explosive and properly conditioned for pitching. Your body will learn to move itself and external objects (weights, bats, balls) faster.

Run sprints most of the time, but distance once in a while, and you'll have the best of both worlds. If you like distance running, use moderation. If you don't, stick to sprinting.

Too many coaches will say, "Only do this 100% of the time!" Occasionally, firm rules are sound. However, in the strength and conditioning world, firm rules rarely apply. The reason? Everyone is different. What works for some won't work for others. What we want to start with is what works for most.

Sprints are great for pitchers. And while distance running isn't, it also won't kill a pitcher if he goes on a 20 minute run once per week. A pitcher's velocity may jump from 88 to 90mph if he concentrates on sprinting regularly over a long period of time – he'll teach his body to become more explosive, athletic and dynamic. And yet, his velocity certainly won't drop from 90 back down to 88 if he decides to mix in a distance run here and there. Almost anything is OK in small doses – cookies, ice cream, and distance running all included. Here are some guidelines for integrating running into your plan:

Spend Most of Your Time (Up to 5 Days Per Week)

100% Effort Sprints: 10yd, 20yd, 30yd, 40yd, 50yd, 60yd

Use these shorter distances to build maximum speed. Sprints are taxing and mentally difficult to stay motivated to perform, so aim to complete your sprint session feeling good – tired, but with gas left in the tank.

You're not training to be a sprinter, so 6-10 longer sprints or 10-15 shorter ones should be plenty. Use higher rest intervals, 60-120 seconds between sprints. Rule of thumb: feel fully rested before your next sprint.

A Little Less Time (2-3 Short Workouts Per Week)

85-100% Effort Runs: 100yd, 200yd, 400yd

These longer distances, run at a near-sprint, are incredibly difficult. And, as mentioned above, you're not training to be an Olympian. As such, if you go out and run six 400s as hard as you can, in a few weeks or months you'll hate running and give up altogether. The goal should always be to train in manageable chunks and do it again the next day, not try to be a hero every day of the week. Your author made the mistake of burning himself out with soul-crushing workouts for 7 or 8 years. Don't do it! Train optimally, not maximally.

1600 total yards is a long workout if running at near 85-100% effort, and 800-1200yds is a good, average length workout. Rest is ideally 1-2 minutes for 100s and 200s or 2-3 minutes for 400s.

Infrequently (Maybe Once Per Week)

50-75% Effort Runs: 15-25 minutes

These fall into the aerobic, or distance category and won't do much to help performance, but will condition the heart and provide some mental and physical benefits slightly outside the scope of pitching. It's a good thing to mix things up, and some days it is difficult to summon the mental energy to sprint.

Getting the Most Out of Training

Understand that there is no magic bullet, and even hard work today isn't a magic bullet; what matters most is a body of work. What this means is that training hard for one day, for a few weeks or even a few months won't make a pitcher into anything special. He may get better, but he won't change the direction of his career.

Those with average physical ability are capable of extraordinary things if, and only if, they devote their lives to training – *needing* to reach their dreams. This takes years of consistent hard work, day in and day out. And, for one to continue to train hard for 5, 10 or 20 years, the training must be manageable. "Manageable" means something different for everyone, but it generally means the minimum effective dose – train hard enough to get quality work in for that day, but not so hard that one wears down over time either physically or mentally. Ambitious young athletes sometimes want to be the one who does the most, who works the hardest (your author included).

However, training reaches points of physically diminishing returns, pushing past which will only serve to wear the athlete down. Once a player is sufficiently fast, sufficiently big, sufficiently strong, he need only maintain that level to perform at his best on the mound. To suffer extra to continually try to break squat records, timed run records, or whatever, misses the point of training. The goal is to reach elite performance and be optimally prepared to pitch. Your author, for example, can squat over 400 pounds. Increasing that number to 500 pounds is unlikely to provide any further benefit to pitching. Increasing his squat from 185 to 400+ over a period of many years, however, provided a large benefit. The increased leg strength, size, and explosiveness all contributed to an increase in throwing velocity.

Train hard, but train optimally. Break intense training into short sessions that can be maintained over a lifetime. Work hard, be consistent, don't miss training sessions, and leave some gas in the tank for the drive home.

CHAPTER 15
ARM STRENGTHENING

Pitching, over time, has a near-100% injury rate. The throwing arm needs a balance of strength and joint stability to protect itself from the high stresses produced on the mound. A good arm strengthening routine for the rotator cuff, scapula stabilizers and forearms will hopefully prevent injury, or, at the very least, delay it.

The Big Picture

If you aren't taking care of your arm, which will be hereto defined as performing 20-30 minutes of throwing arm strengthening at least 4 days per week, then arm pain and injury is in your future. It's only a question of when.

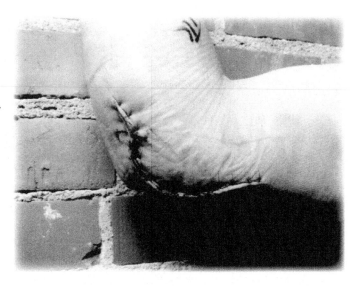

The throwing motion is unnatural, stressful and destructive. The only way to delay, and hopefully prevent, injury is by keeping the involved muscles strong, stable and balanced. The sad reality is that most baseball organizations and high schools do not provide strengthening programs or any guidelines for preventive arm care. So, it's up to the informed coach, parent and athlete to take the matter into his own hands. A good starting place is with basic knowledge of the structures involved.

Fundamental Throwing Arm Anatomy – The Rotator Cuff

The rotator cuff is the most important group of muscles involved in the overhand throw. While many young athletes point to the front of their shoulder when asked to identify the location of the rotator cuff, the "cuff" muscles are actually located on the back of the shoulder. All four muscles comprising the rotator cuff group originate on the shoulder blade. The rotator cuff acts to stabilize the humerus bone (the upper arm) in the shoulder joint, as well as provide muscular force in accelerating and decelerating the throwing arm. The four muscles of the rotator cuff are:

- Subscapularis (Internally rotates the arm)
- Teres Minor (Externally rotates the arm)
- Infraspinatus (Externally rotates the arm)
- Supraspinatus (Lifts the arm)

Internal rotation is rotation of the arm toward the plate, providing acceleration to the baseball. The prime mover of internal rotation (the muscle providing the most force) is the subscapularis muscle.

External Rotation is rotation of the arm away from the plate, providing the force to lay the arm back and decelerate it after release. The prime mover of external rotation is the teres minor, followed by the infraspinatus.

The supraspinatus is active to help stabilize the shoulder and help lift and decelerate the arm once the pitch has been released.

Why the Rotator Cuff is Important

The rotator cuff has two main jobs during a throw:
1. Keep the upper arm firmly centered in the shoulder socket
2. Provide muscular force to accelerate and decelerate the arm

We want a very strong rotator cuff that can provide both high accelerative and decelerative forces, as well as stabilize the arm in the shoulder socket. Stronger muscles providing acceleration to the baseball obviously means higher pitch velocities.

But, the arm must have relative balance in the muscles that decelerate the arm after release (the external rotators) to prevent the arm from literally flying out of the socket. The most commonly injured rotator cuff muscles are the external rotators and supraspinatus, because they are often too weak to handle the stresses created by hard-throwing pitchers. The old saying is, "a car is only as fast as its brakes," meaning that injury is certain if the arm can't properly decelerate the force that it can create.

Lastly, the head of the humerus bone must be held firmly in the socket throughout the duration of the throw. This is the rotator cuff's most fundamental job – preventing the bone from bouncing around in the joint, causing tendons, ligaments and other passive tissues to stretch too far, fray or tear. A stable shoulder can handle much higher speeds and pitch counts before breaking down.

Fundamental Throwing Arm Anatomy – Muscles of the Forearm

Knowing the individual forearm muscles isn't overly important. What is important? Simply understanding that they work in groups. The muscles in the anterior forearm compartment are referred to as the wrist flexor/pronator mass. The muscles in the posterior compartment are referred to as the wrist extensors. Each compartment controls the wrist in different ways. I will attempt to explain the actions without use of medical terminology. For the actions below, assume the hand is held out in front of the body.

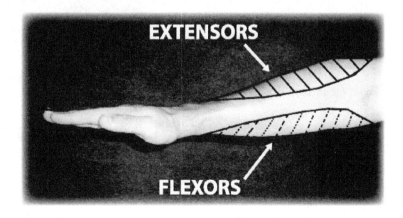

Forearm flexor/pronator mass produces these movements:

1. Flexes wrist (curls wrist inward)

2. Pronates wrist (rotates palm away from face)

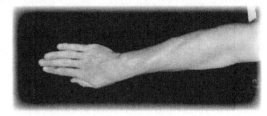

3. Ulnar-deviates the wrist (moves pinky toward the arm)

Forearm Extensors produce these movements:

1. Extends wrist (pulls wrist backward)

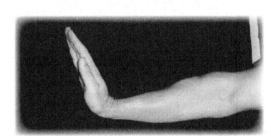

2. Radial-deviates the wrist (moves thumb toward the arm)

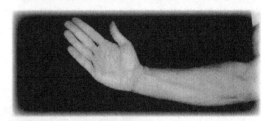

3. Supinates wrist (rotates palm toward the body)

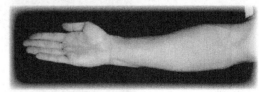

Why the Forearms are Important

The forearm muscles control the wrist and hand, which are the last body parts controlling the baseball. The hand helps to catapult the ball at release and amplify arm velocity, and stronger forearm muscles can increase force on the baseball at release.

Stronger hands and forearms may also increase dexterity and allow a pitcher to more finely tune the movement in all of his different pitches.

Lastly, the forearm flexor/pronator mass crosses the elbow joint. Because of this, this muscle group provides support for the Ulnar Collateral Ligament (UCL), the ligament that, when torn, requires Tommy John Surgery. The forearm muscles contract to keep the joint from spreading apart. Without forearm muscles helping to keep the elbow joint held tightly together, pitchers would tear their UCL at very low velocities. Stronger forearm muscles provide increased support for the UCL and thus play a key role in preventing injury.

Fundamental Throwing Arm Anatomy – The Deltoid Muscles

The deltoids are the large, round shoulder muscles prominent in basketball players. They help to lift the throwing arm and play a lesser role in stabilizing the shoulder and decelerating the arm. They have the potential to be quite strong. Because of this, the deltoids can overpower the rotator cuff if trained too heavily, resulting in some negative adaptations for the pitcher.

Why the Deltoids are Important

Pitchers should not heavily train their deltoids. If the deltoids are too big and strong, they pull the upper arm to the top of the shoulder joint. Without getting too technical, this results in slight misalignment of the ball and socket as the arm moves and rotates during the throw. Balanced shoulder musculature that pulls the humerus equally in all directions keeps the shoulder tissues in optimal condition. Overpowering deltoids can disrupt this balance by pulling the arm very hard in an upward direction.

Fundamental Throwing Arm Anatomy – The Scapula Stabilizers

The scapula, or shoulder blade, must be held firmly against the rib cage as it glides in all directions. Strength and balance must be achieved in the following muscles:

- Rhomboids
- Trapezius (upper, middle and lower fibers)
- Serratus anterior
- Levator scapulae

During movement, these muscles are responsible for moving the shoulder blade and providing it with stability on the ribcage. Strength and balance among them will place the shoulder blade in a biomechanically optimal position for movement of the arm.

Why the Scapula Stabilizers Are Important

When imbalance and weakness occurs in any of the muscles that stabilize the shoulder blade, it can "wing" off the rib cage and/or become misaligned in static posture. These changes alter the biomechanics of the throwing motion in ways that increase stress on the shoulder and elbow. nstability of the scapula stabilizers is a very common finding among amateur pitchers, one that is a chief culprit of arm pain.

Recommendations for Strengthening the Throwing Shoulder

There are many good strength coaches and physical therapists who are capable of creating quality arm strengthening programs. Providing a program worthy of print is too big a task for the narrow scope of this book. "Cookie-cutter" programs of adequate brevity would be inadequate in quality for the wide range of strength and ability levels of players reading this book. The best course of action is the following:

Seek an evaluation from a local physical therapist with expert knowledge and experience with baseball players. Find out who provides care to the local professional baseball team and book an appointment with him or her. A good assessment will address at least the following:
- Rotator cuff strength
- Shoulder blade alignment
- Shoulder blade movement
- Range of motion
- Static and dynamic posture
- Individual body structure
- Shoulder internal and external rotation range of motion

Ask the therapist to create a program specifically for you based on the evaluation. Follow it and follow up with the physical therapist to ensure progress is being made. Once he or she is happy with your progress, maintain it by continuing to stay diligent.

If an in-depth assessment and personal attention is beyond one's budget or capability, the next best course of action is a baseball-specific arm-strengthening program. Many can be found commercially, so do some investigating to find the right program for your needs. Warbird Academy Warbands are a great choice, as are Jaeger Sports J-Bands. Both are high-quality products designed to meet the needs of baseball players. However,

using latex bands, while convenient and prevalent, are not the only tool for strengthening the throwing arm. Many quality exercises are performed using dumbbells or bodyweight resistance.

Recommendations for Strengthening the Forearms

As mentioned in chapter 14, strengthening the hands and forearms is best accomplished by holding heavy objects in the hands. Weighted carries are among the best bang-for-buck choices to build stronger forearms and hands. A search on warbirdacademy.com, YouTube or Google for "farmers walk" will provide examples and guidelines for integrating weighted carries into a strength program.

The best resource for more specific forearm training is provided on warbirdacademy.com by searching for "tommy john rehab." Because Tommy John surgery involves cutting into the forearm flexor/pronator mass, and the forearm muscles protect the reconstructed ligament, strengthening the forearms is a huge aspect of the rehab process. Preemptively performing rehab is one of the best ways to ward off the very injury the rehab was designed for. Full guidelines for performing the forearm strengthening exercises provided by the world's best surgeons and physical therapists is clearly explained on warbirdacademy.com

CHAPTER 16

FREQUENTLY HAD DISCUSSIONS

We've had these talks before; we all need some tough love and some eye-opening discussion about the realities of this pastime of ours.

I throw 85 mph. It's my dream to pitch in the major leagues. Jamie Moyer, Livan Hernandez, and Greg Maddux all threw in the mid-80s. How do I get noticed?

You will never make it to the majors throwing below, on average, 90mph. There is a tremendous correlation in major league success and velocity – nearly all the "big name" pitchers are also the harder throwers in the league. Fangraphs.com will corroborate this.

Also, Maddux, Moyer, and Hernandez all threw in the low-90s in the first part of their careers. They learned how to get major leaguers out, even as their velocity declined with age, so they stayed in the game. Very few players throw less than 89mph, on average, in the majors, and almost no one gets signed in the first place without being capable of averaging 90mph.

You need to work on making your arm stronger if you wish to realize your dream.

I've heard that strength training is bad for pitchers. Is this true?

No. Strength training is the best way to increase velocity and durability. There's a strong correlation between bodyweight and velocity, but many people ignore this, thinking that a "lean frame" is the ideal way to throw hard. The pitchers you see in the big leagues who are skinny are, well, genetic freaks. For every skinny pitcher who throws gas, there are 100,000 skinny amateurs who can't break a pane of glass. One thing to note about the majors is how big most players are: They're big for a reason, and if you're not tall, you should work really hard getting stronger and more muscular.

The reason strength training gets a bad reputation is because most athletes lift weights with inadequate – or no – supervision. A qualified strength coach who knows the needs of baseball players should construct and supervise a strength training program. Simply going to the local commercial gym and/or doing football-style lifting at school is unlikely to yield any benefit; I see it all the time. Furthermore, the time for very intense, serious strength training is the off-season. While in-season strength training for maintenance is important, great players are made in the offseason.

I throw a really good knuckleball. R.A. Dickey won the Cy Young. How can I get a college to notice my knuckeball-throwing ability?

No. You're not R.A. Dickey. Here is why:

He threw 95mph when he was drafted, and was not converted into a knuckleballer until many years later in the minor leagues. Scouts do not initially sign knuckleballers; they are converted once they fail as "regular" pitchers. There are almost no knuckleball pitchers at the collegiate or pro level. R.A. Dickey is an exceptionally rare example.

Throwing knuckleballs in games as an amateur is a wasteful activity, and if I were scouting a pitcher who did so, he would be crossed off of my list. It's not a pitch that scouts are interested in for an amateur, and a college coach would never give scholarship money to a knuckleballer over a traditional pitcher.

Spend your time perfecting command, fastball velocity and traditional offspeed pitches like the curveball, changeup and slider.

I throw a fastball, changeup, curveball, cutter and slider. Oh – and a forkball. Roy Halladay throws five or six pitches and I want a big arsenal like his.

No. Most D-1 prospects throw a hard fastball and a very good second pitch, with a mediocre third pitch; most pro pitchers have the same. Those who make it in the big leagues have three exceptional pitches, and only sometimes four.

The reality is that if you throw five pitches as a high-schooler, at least three of them are garbage. I've seen it time and time again. Scrap all but your strongest three – typically a fastball, changeup and either a curveball or slider.

The reasoning for this is simple – the only people who can devote precious pitches to developing a fourth or fifth offering are those who already have a fantastic arsenal. If your whole repertoire needs work, we would break down a typical 40-pitch bullpen as such:

8 Fastballs
8 Changeups
8 Curves
8 Sliders
8 Cutters

You can't throw seven bullpens a week. Rather, two bullpens is the norm. So now you're only throwing 16 of each per week, which is not nearly enough to improve a pitch.

Additionally, how do you know when to use which pitch? There's no point having five pitches if they all don't have specific uses. And, middle and high school hitters are not nearly good enough for a pitcher to need five pitches to get them out. A well-located fastball and sharp curveball or quality changeup will absolutely dominate a high school team; there's really no need for more.

The major goal is repetition, and it takes thousands upon thousands of throws to develop a pitch to the point of being collegiate baseball quality. And college coaches are only interested in pitchers who have the stuff to get college hitters out. So, scrap the five mediocre pitches for three good ones. "Jack of all trades but master of none" is what we want to avoid.

When should I start throwing a curveball or slider?

Freshman year in high school, depending on your physical maturity. It's a safe idea to wait until the growth plates are closed, because researchers still don't know enough about how breaking balls interact with the arm.

The only pitchers in college and pro baseball who lack a changeup in their arsenal are eighth inning guys and closers – the hardest throwers in the game. They don't throw changeups because an 87mph changeup is often a gift to a hitter who can't catch up with 96-99mph. Nearly all other pro and high-level collegiate pitchers throw a changeup.

Only about 40 men in the big leagues average above 94mph. Out of 300 million Americans, we can safely say that only 0.000016% of the population does not throw above 94mph, and thus does not need a changeup in their arsenal. Chances are… you need a changeup.

So, it's my recommendation that since you'll need a changeup anyway, spend your open-growth-plate years throwing the changeup rather than a curveball. It will pay dividends later on when your arm feels healthier and your changeup is much more advanced relative to your peers.

I'm really slow to the plate, but I don't allow many baserunners. Do I need to bother with a slide step or faster delivery?

Yes, you do. Many pitchers get comfortable in slow deliveries because they find success that way. But, the standard all pitchers should hold themselves to is that of higher-level players – collegiate and professionals. Though it may not be much of an issue for a high school pitcher to deliver to the plate in 1.7 seconds, it will turn scouts off to him and will cost him runs at higher levels. Pitchers need to develop next-level mechanics, not current-level mechanics. This means sometimes developing skills that aren't completely necessary for success today, but will be crucial down the road.

Are other sports good for my development as a pitcher?

Yes and no. The better pitchers are always the more athletic pitchers. Playing other sports helps develop and hone athleticism, speed, agility and body control. This can be a great thing for young athletes, especially.

But, if you're reaching sophomore or junior year in high school and aren't the biggest, baddest ballplayer around (be honest please) then playing a second or third sport is likely taking time away from maximizing your pitching potential. If athlete A spends 12 solid months training solely to improve his pitching, and athlete B spends just four months on his pitching, who do you think will improve more in that calendar year? Obviously athlete A. Although the other eight months for athlete B were devoted to basketball and football, which are good for athleticism in general, those sports won't carry over to the specific act of throwing a well-located fastball at high velocity.

So, playing other sports at a young age is a great thing. But, if baseball is your long-term passion, look long and hard at whether or not playing other sports is preventing you from reaching your full potential.

What's an appropriate pitch count for a game?

It's important to understand that although pitch counts are somewhat arbitrary, they still should be observed out of caution. 100 is a nice, round number but is in no way tied to physiology. Every pitcher is different in his capacity for pitching, but we need to focus on making sure pitchers aren't overused or abused. Overuse is still the strongest correlating factor to pitching injuries – the more competitive pitching per year, the higher likelihood an injury will occur.

For this reason, it's best to limit pitchers to the following rough guidelines. It's always better to be safe than sorry.

Age 17+: 100 pitches or less
Age 15-17: 80 pitches or less
Ages 13-14: 60 pitches or less
Ages 12 and under: 40 pitches or less

If a pitcher is playing the field in between his outings, especially at a throwing-intensive position such as shortstop or catcher, his pitch counts should be limited even further. The arm will have less ability to recover between outings if he is throwing hard from other positions. Remember that pro pitchers never play other positions.

Additionally, for every 20 pitches thrown, at least one day of rest should be observed before the next outing. I recommend additional rest days added if the pitcher is also playing another position on "rest" days.

How many months of the year should a pitcher pitch competitively?

For amateurs not yet in college, the answer is five or less. Two or three months should be taken completely off of all types of throwing (a great time to work on mechanical drills and strength training), and the other four or five months should be devoted to practicing pitching skills and throwing in a non-competitive environment. The pitcher needs to throw a lot to improve and develop the velocity needed to play at higher levels. But, this velocity is better developed in a training environment rather than a game environment. More games means more maximal effort pitching that will increase the likelihood of injury. And lastly, while game experience is very important, mechanical improvements don't "take" while playing. More downtime from games means more time to improve skills, arm and overall strength, and mechanics.

- Epilogue -

Starting at age 18, in 2004, I spent all of my free time trying to find ways to become a better pitcher. I wasn't all that good - I was the ninth best pitcher on my team as a freshman in college and average around 80 miles per hour. But, I wasn't okay going out that way. I started asking questions and experimenting on myself to figure out what would work best, to most quickly drive me up the baseball mountain.

When I opened my own strength training and baseball academy in 2010, I started applying the principles I learned to those I trained. The key word in that sentence is principles. Too many coaches are dogmatic and attempt to mold every pitcher into a carbon copy of a themselves, a successful major leaguer or some other archetype of good pitching. This is not the way.

Working with hundreds of aspiring athletes every year, it's amazing to see the variance in everyone's unique anatomy. No one moves the same way, no one's bones are shaped the same way, and no one's muscles respond to stimuli in the same way. Everyone is different.

So when writing this book, I didn't want to create a manual on how to create clones of myself or any other professional pitcher. Rather, I wanted to give you, the reader, my take on the biggest, most important aspects of pitching that need to be internalized and practiced. Big league hitters will tell you that hitting a stationary baseball off of a tee is the most important drill to their success. Pitching is this same way – with so many wacky and complex pitching drills out there, how are we to know what works what should occupy the bulk of our time. I hope after reading this book, you have a more clear understanding of the drills I feel will provide high-level mastery of pitching for almost everyone.

The bottom line is that every pro pitcher comes from a different town, which means he had different coaches from his bullpen mate. So, with all of these different philosophies and training styles, how is it that every pro pitcher exhibits 90% of the same mechanical traits, body positions and pitching maxims? It's because most of what makes a good pitcher isn't a secret, isn't overly complicated, and is largely accessible to everyone, should they seek it.

The Dominicans are a great example. They provide the world with more major leaguers per capita than any country. Is it because they have massive biomechanics laboratories, the best fields, trainers, and coaches? Certainly not – much of the country lives in poverty. The common thread appears to be practice – all of these aspiring major leaguers spend all day at the ballpark practicing their skills with astronomically high repetition. Practice makes perfect, and the Dominicans likely practice more than anyone. At the end of all that practice, they end up pretty darned good. Weird, huh? Practice produces good ballplayers!

So please, take the information in this book with a grain of salt. If some of the drills seem boring or remedial, that's because they're suppose to be, because simplicity is the best solution when it comes to actions that need to practiced perfectly hundreds of thousands of times. I firmly believe that if you practice the biggest, most important aspects of any skill with very high repetition, you'll end up better than nearly everyone and realize along the way that hard work and focus is the only "secret" that the professionals possess.

And, if a solution that you require isn't found in this book, I'll pass along to you what one of my mentors, Roye Templeton, passed along to me many years ago. I had just learned that I would need Tommy John surgery and that because of it my college career was over. Simply, he stated:

"A resolute man will find a way."

Your fate is always in your hands if you're willing to get back up, dust yourself off, and keep grinding. Easy isn't what you want, anyway.

Photo Credits

Made in the USA
Coppell, TX
12 March 2023

14155329R00122